ORIGEN AND HIS WORK

ORIGEN
AND HIS WORK

BY

EUGÈNE DE FAYE

*Directeur d'Études à l'École Pratique des Hautes Études,
Professeur d'Histoire Ecclésiastique à la Faculté
Protestante de Théologie, Paris; Doctor of
Divinity of Aberdeen University*

AUTHORISED TRANSLATION BY
FRED ROTHWELL

WIPF & STOCK · Eugene, Oregon

Wipf and Stock Publishers
199 W 8th Ave, Suite 3
Eugene, OR 97401

Origen and His Work
By De Faye, Eugene and Rothwell, Fred
ISBN 13: 978-1-60608-278-2
Publication date 2/11/2011
Previously published by Columbia UP, 1923

PREFACE

LAST year (1925) the Olaus Petri Endowment greatly honoured the author by inviting him to deliver a few lectures on Origen at the University of Upsala. It was agreed that they should be published and we now offer them to the public exactly as they were delivered.

There could be no question of expounding the entire thought of Origen in eight conferences. We have been compelled to pass over more than one important doctrine—for instance, his ideas on the Gnosis. Still less was it possible to set forth in these lectures the enormous mass of documents upon which our exposition of the theology of Origen is based.

All this is reserved for our second volume on Origen, now in course of preparation. All the same, it is a peculiar pleasure to offer our friends in Sweden the first fruits, if such a term may be used, of the large volume we hope to publish subsequently.

May we be permitted to express the lively sense of gratitude we feel to Archbishop Soederblom, who on this occasion graciously set forth how greatly he has always esteemed French science, and also to the public of this University of Upsala, where such solid instruction is given by so many illustrious masters.

EUGÈNE DE FAYE.

CONTENTS

	PAGE
PREFACE	7
INTRODUCTION	13
THE CHARACTER OF ORIGEN'S WRITINGS, HIS THOUGHT AND METHOD	33
THE DOCTRINE OF GOD	55
COSMOLOGY	77
CHRISTOLOGY	99
THE DOCTRINE OF REDEMPTION	121
FINAL THINGS	145
CONCLUSIONS	169
INDEX	189

INTRODUCTION

INTRODUCTION

ORIGEN'S active life and work belong to the first fifty years of the third century, a period which has largely been neglected—even despised. Historians regard it as marking the death struggle of the world of antiquity and the decline of the Empire. Ominous signs announce the approaching catastrophe. Artists lament the decadence of art. Literature no longer produces a single masterpiece. Philosophers compare this age with the classic age of philosophy—and disparage it accordingly; they begin to manifest interest in the third century only when Plotinus appears on the scene.

This is a rather superficial, and therefore ultra-simple, view of the situation. It should be remembered that this century is linked on to the preceding one; all those tendencies of feeling and thought that are in germ during the second century, came to fruition in the time of Origen and Plotinus. The result is a potent ferment of ideas, a bitter contest of opposing doctrines, a spiritual activity of the human soul that is both manifold and intense.

We shall see this if we cast a rapid glance at the philosophical and religious activity of the time. There is taking place an unexpected blossoming of religions and devout cults that have their origin in Egypt, Babylon, Persia, Syria and Asia Minor. The syncretistic cults have considerable vogue. The old mysteries of Eleusis, of Samothrace and elsewhere have been revived and are more popular than ever. In a subsequent lecture, we shall have an opportunity of explaining the nature of this religious renaissance.

If we study the philosophers, we are struck by the mental activity displayed, e.g. by Plutarch and his followers. The circle of friends around him range the entire field of philosophy from Epicurus to Chrysippus. His treatises *Ad Colotem* and *De Stoicorum Repugnantiis* testify to a profound knowledge of the philosophical teachings which they criticise, as well as of their history. Other treatises show him to be engaged on new problems which excite his enthusiasm as much as did the old problems in the case of the philosophers who preceded him. If we interrogate the Stoics of the time, from Musonius down to Marcus Aurelius, we note the same intensity of thought—thought very different from that of the early masters, though no less original and profound. Far from declining, philosophy now acquires a degree of influence it has not hitherto known. It becomes popular, has its own orators and propagandists. Dion Prusaensis, Maximus Tyrius and many others popularise its maxims and its ideals. And finally, after Ammonius Saccas, Plotinus and his first disciples endow philosophy with an incomparable halo of glory.

No less remarkable is the activity of thought among the Christians of the second and third centuries. About the middle of the former appear the first Christian theologians, for as such must we regard the classic Gnostics of the period. Basilides and his son Isidorus, Valentinus and his disciples, Ptolemaeus, Heracleon, Marcion and Apelles still belong to the Church. It is as Christian thinkers that they deal with the problems of God and providence, of the origin and destiny of the Cosmos, of Christology and the intermediaries between the absolute God and the Cosmos, of redemption, of revelation—as regards both the Old Testament and Jesus and his apostles. In the third century, the Gnostic sects secede from the Church and form themselves into associations, into veritable mysteries; the Marcionites into churches. Never were they more formidable to the Church.

In these sects—such as that of the *Philosophumena* of Hippolytus or those revealed to us in Coptic documents—the ferment of ideas and tendencies is extreme. Speculations, exegeses, contributions from syncretistic religions, expiatory rites, recipes for salvation, asceticism, obscene practices: here are to be found all the aspiration and imagination, all the pseudo-science of the age.

The Christians faithful to tradition are brimming over with ideas. Apologists like Aristides, Justin, Tatian and others give the signal. They have made considerable advance upon the early Christian writers, Clemens Romanus, Ignatius, the Shepherd of Hermas. Theology and the interpretation of the Scriptures make their appearance with Irenaeus and Hippolytus, while Clement and Origen herald a magnificent expansion of Christian thought. Even in the West, where mentality is practical and alien to dogmatic speculation and a bold allegorical exegesis, thought and discussion are prevalent. The moral treatises of Tertullian prove that the Church of Carthage discussed all essential questions dealing with conduct and the Christian life. Here, the debates seem to have been very lively, the opinions extremely varied.

In effect, the third century is far from dull or mediocre. We can trace four great streams of aspirations and tendencies: the syncretistic religions, philosophy, Gnosticism, and finally

Christianity. They seem to assert an approximately equal influence; it is difficult to foresee which will prevail. Ardent is the struggle in this century.

Truly vital and fruitful epochs generally have a problem of their own, one that in different degrees occupies the minds of all. What is the problem of this period? An essentially religious one. In all circles, whether Christian, non-Christian, or Jew, it is religion that absorbs attention. On the other hand, the culture of antiquity still holds sway. The main problem, therefore, for every reflecting mind, is to attune one's beliefs to one's thought, one's mysticism—whatever its nature—to one's philosophy. And this is abundantly demonstrated by facts. Look at Plutarch, a philosopher to the very marrow. He is thoroughly acquainted with every system and method, and has boundless veneration for the greatest of philosophers, Socrates and Plato. All the same, he cannot detach himself from the popular religion. This is more than a matter of feeling in his case; he has genuine religious beliefs. He has faith in oracles and divination, and is convinced of the presence and activity, amongst men, of inferior deities whom he calls "daimons", He looks upon providence as self-evident, and so is unable to reject the positive religions; at the very least, they seem to him to contain an element of truth, or rather the most sublime truth in mythical form. Consequently it is for him a necessity, both of feeling and of thought, to reconcile his beliefs with his philosophy. This is a problem the solution of which he passionately sought in his writings, *De sera numinis vindicta*, *De oraculorum defectu*, *De ei*, and more particularly in his *De Iside et Osiride*.

Epictetus the Stoic also manifests the same preoccupation. Of all the philosophers of his day, he is perhaps the one whose soul is most profoundly tinged with mysticism. He has a way of speaking of God—whatever name he gives to Him—as though He were a person in his very presence. To remain at the post God has assigned him is the first of duties. The last occupation of his life on earth will be to sing to God. On the other hand, even though he does not take up metaphysics, discourse upon the Cosmos, its origin, continuance and destiny, and but seldom argues as a Stoic dialectitian, he is nevertheless imbued with the essential principles of Stoicism. This latter is ever in the background of his thought. His distinctively moral philosophy could not be understood apart from the doctrine of the immanence of God in the Cosmos, of that of the universal law of the Cosmos, of the idea of man's relationship to God, of the principle of the solidarity (κοινωνία) of mankind. His intellectual achievement consists precisely in having so powerfully and completely blended into one his philosophy, his morality and his religion. The whole of his work is an admirable religious and moral interpretation of Stoicism. Another instance of the reconciliation of a philosophy with religious beliefs is found in the Olympic discourse of Dion Prusaensis. This is an eloquent interpretation in philosophical terms of the idea which Phidias, according to the orator, had conceived of Zeus. The man of philosophy and the man of religion meet on the common ground of art.

If we consider the Gnostic theologians of the second century, we find that they also, though in another way, attempt to find the solution of the same problem. Naturally they attribute slight importance to the Christian traditions; they claim to possess esoteric traditions that are far superior. It is a fact, all the same, that they hold certain religious beliefs which manifestly originate in Christianity, such as the idea of the fall, that of redemption, that of the saving mission of Christ, and others. These beliefs they sometimes blended with Platonic, Stoic and Pythagorean doctrines, or even with syncretistic conceptions. From this union came the system of Valentinus, and the systems of the Gnostics of the *Philosophumena*.

The Christians of the great Church itself end in allowing themselves to be beset by the same cares and preoccupations. Harnack lifted the veil upon the real Christianity of the second century, showing from ancient documents the true character of their beliefs, which were very powerful and vital. As Renan had already stated, these were the beliefs of the masses, expressed in popular language. What could be more uncouth than the notions of the Shepherd of Hermas? No wonder that people about the year A.D. 130 did not understand either the theology of the Apostle Paul or the Logos of the fourth Gospel. Was it possible that Christianity should remain at this stage? The necessity of defending itself speedily compelled it to self-expression in more refined language. To prove how harmless were its beliefs, it saw itself forced to compare them with certain philosophical doctrines, and to maintain that they did not differ from them so much as was imagined; consequently, that they should enjoy the same degree of tolerance as was accorded to philosophy.

The prejudice which did most harm to the Christians was that they were looked upon as low, coarse and uncivilised. When Justin appears before the *praefectus urbi*, the latter manifests the greatest surprise at the idea of a learned man

INTRODUCTION

and a scholar being a Christian. Even at the time of Commodus, when Apollonius appears before *Perennis* and the Senate, his judges cannot overcome their amazement at discovering that such a philosopher as he was had espoused the absurd beliefs of the Christians. To overcome these prejudices, the more intellectual among the Christians were absolutely compelled to formulate the Christian faith in more or less philosophical terms. This was attempted by Justin, Tatian and Athenagoras.

No sooner was Christianity bent upon expanding into more intellectual circles, than the necessity of expressing its beliefs in more literary language and more philosophical formulas made itself felt. How could men, themselves the product of the schools of philosophy, when once they became Christians, prevent themselves from desiring to convert friends and co-disciples to their new faith? Should they happen to be at Athens, Alexandria, or Pergamus, they could not even converse with others on the ideas most dear to them if they did not speak the language of the schools and set forth Christianity as the only true philosophy. Consequently, conditions that it was useless to strive against, must sooner or later induce the Christians to tolerate—and speedily to seek—relations with philosophy. In their turn, they found themselves faced with the problem which confronted every contemporary thinker.

Clement of Alexandria was the first Christian of the great Church to understand the signs of the times; indeed, he was in a better position than others to discern them. He was at the head of the catechetical school of Alexandria. His writings, which were nothing but the summary of his teaching, give us at all events indirect information regarding his pupils. These were assuredly cultured young men, even students at the schools of philosophy. Some were Christian, others still pagan when they came to the Didascaleion. They were not long before becoming converted to Christianity. Clement first endeavours to train them for Christian living; afterwards he teaches the Christian philosophy to a select few. He wishes them to become accomplished "Gnostics", i.e. Christians who possess the true science and are trained in the practice of brotherly love. His perfect Christian unites love and the Gnosis in one and the same ideal. If such was Clement's programme, it was not given to him to realise it to the full. To a considerable extent he found it necessary to justify, to Christians whose minds he filled with disquiet, the use he made of philosophy and the place he assigned to it in his teaching. It was Origen his disciple to whom was reserved the credit and glory of

INTRODUCTION

indissolubly linking vital Christian beliefs on to Greek philosophy, which then held sovereign sway over the minds of men.

Origen was born in the year A.D. 185.[1] At the time of his birth, his parents, in all probability, were still pagan. This explains why they gave him a name which signified that he had been born on the anniversary of Horus. Probably many other children were named Origen (born of Horus) for the same reason. He was perhaps seven or eight years of age when his father Leonides, and all his family, became Christians, so that Origen was brought up in a family of ardent neophytes. The impression was indelible; he remained a fervent believer during the whole of his life. At the outset, it was his wish to hand himself over to his persecutors; in the year A.D. 235 he wrote his *Exhortation to Martyrdom*; at the age of seventy, during the Decian persecution, he made his confession of faith with heroical constancy and endured tortures which appear to have shattered his health and caused his death.

Leonides, finding that his son was gifted to an exceptional degree, gave him an excellent education and sent him to the catechetical school of which Clement was at the head.

[1] This is the date upon which I have finally fixed. See my first volume of *Origène, sa vie, sa pensée et son œuvre*, page 5.

Our future theologian was first taught in Alexandria. In everything that is not purely Christian he is a true son of that city. For five centuries Alexandria was the most learned city in the civilised world; every science and school of thought was there represented. Two libraries and the museum constituted an admirable centre of noble culture. The subjects taught included mathematics, astronomy, natural history and geography. The Ptolemies organised regular scientific expeditions; there were numerous professorships of rhetoric and literature. In the libraries, students commented on the ancient authors and explained many a text by the allegorical method. The poets themselves were men of learning; there were masters of arts and crafts. Lastly, the schools of philosophy enjoyed real popularity. Ammonius Saccas appears to have exercised a powerful influence upon the youth of the time. Origen attended his classes, and Plotinus was his pupil for a number of years. We can imagine what must have been the intellectual atmosphere of such an environment. Origen was steeped in it; he took full advantage of the resources offered by this truly university town. Considering the age in which he lived, the knowledge he acquired was encyclopaedic. It was extremely varied, though it was philosophy that he appears to have studied more particularly. Like most of the young philosophers of his day, he confined his reading to what might be called the positive philosophies, to Plato, Aristotle, the Stoics. He felt nothing but disdain for critics and sceptics, for Pyrrho and the New Academy. He was thoroughly acquainted with contemporary representatives of the great schools, with Platonists, Pythagoreans and Stoics. To satisfy the requirements of exegesis, he makes use of his Gnostic predecessors, of Heracleon for instance, author of the first commentary on the Gospel of John. He was well acquainted with Valentinus and Marcion. Naturally, he possessed a most minute knowledge of the Scriptures. His faultless memory immediately called up any Bible text he needed. At the same time, he was acquainted with those writings in the Greek language, still few in number, which the Christians had brought out. Of all the Christians of his day, he was the most eminent; his reputation was widespread and well established. Porphyry expresses regret that such a man should be inveigled by the miserable ravings of the Jews and the Christians.

It was in no haphazard fashion that Origen approached the problem of the relations between faith and philosophy; one might even say that, at first, he avoids it. Eusebius actually claims that, in his fervour as a Christian doctor, he sold the manuscripts of ancient authors which he had copied himself. Is this information reliable, has he heard it from Pamphilius, for instance? We do not know. What appears certain is that when he re-opens the catechetical school, during the persecution of the Christians in A.D. 203, he wishes to confine himself to interpreting the Scriptures. He seems to have turned the Didascaleion into a Bible school, not confining himself to the rôle of expositor. Amongst his pupils were cultured youths who had already studied philosophy, so that he found himself compelled to discuss Christian doctrines and Bible texts with them. He had to expound, for instance, such teachings regarding God and providence as a young philosopher, like those to whom Plutarch introduces us in his treatise on the tardiness of divine justice, could accept. It was not enough to assert his faith in providence, he had to give philosophical proof of it. Only on this condition could he obtain a hearing. Thus, Origen's early experiences taught him the necessity of interpreting his Christian beliefs in terms of Greek philosophy. To propound a philosophical interpretation of Christianity he regarded as his life work.

This he himself clearly declared in the preface of his *De Principiis*. "The holy apostles", he says, "preachers of the Christian faith, have handed down to us, in the clearest terms, what they look upon as necessary for our faith; they have left it to those who merit the abounding gifts of the spirit, to give rational proof of their affirmations ".[1] At the end of his preface he declares that the affirmations of the faith must become a body of doctrines, in obedience to the express command of God. When Celsus reproaches Christians for disseminating their doctrines chiefly amongst old women, Origen retorts that, on the contrary, when he is speaking to intelligent listeners, he explains to them " all that there is beautiful and divine in our beliefs "; these profounder teachings are not allowed to be given to the simple-minded who would not understand them.[2]

One remark in conclusion. When Clement and Origen attempted to reconcile their faith with their philosophy, they acted in accordance with a necessity of human thought. This necessity has never ceased to make itself felt; it is a real law, imperative upon Christian thought, as indeed upon all religious thought. From the attempt to adapt beliefs to the thought and formulas of philosophy sprang the entire theology of the Councils. Mediaeval theology from Saint Anselm down to Saint Thomas and Saint Bona-

[1] *De Principiis*, praef., chaps. 3 and 10.
[2] *Contra Celsum*, III, 52.

ventura has continued the same attempt with rare vigour and great dialectical subtilty. In the seventeenth century, Descartes, Leibniz, and Malebranche obeyed the same law. In more modern times, what else has been done by such thinkers as Schleiermacher, Ritschl, Secrétan, Sabatier and many others? Clement of Alexandria was therefore right in maintaining that he was justified, even though it might be opposed to the feeling of ordinary believers, in studying philosophy and utilising it in teaching the Christian doctrine, and Origen was right when he united philosophy and Christian belief in formulas—mainly harmonious.

What is too often forgotten is that, with the lapse of time, the problem that beset an Origen or a Plutarch changes its aspect. Neither belief on the one hand, nor philosophy on the other, is immutable. Even mentality becomes modified from age to age. Of a sudden, the problem presents itself in other terms. In the days of Origen, the mentality of the man of culture, whether Christian or pagan, was fundamentally intellectualistic and metaphysical. That which stood in the foreground of all philosophy was a certain transcendent conception of God, an explanation of the Cosmos which had nothing scientific about it, a morality born of the metaphysics that had been adopted, a psychology

INTRODUCTION

which assuredly was not based on the study of human nature. Less than ever did thought form its conceptions from the observation of facts: this it left exclusively to dialectic. The result was a state of mind that was purely intellectualistic and idealistic.

How different from our own! Could one imagine a contrast more radical? To such an extent is this so, that when a modern student reads Origen, he is at first disconcerted, quite out of his bearings. He finds himself in a world of reasonings and abstractions, of verbal distinctions, which he looks upon as altogether unreal. Page follows page without anything to suggest reality. If there were only some grace or charm in these considerations and reflections! However transcendent the metaphysic of Plato, it is tolerated by reason of its plastic beauty.

Our mentality is profoundly realistic, even more than we imagine. For the past two centuries everything has contributed to intensify our sense of reality. We know—and wish to know—nothing but facts. The exact and minute observation of phenomena is the only method we recognise. The progress of natural science and historic disciplines, the study of psychological, social and economic facts, art, literature, and politics, have all contributed to this excessively realistic mentality. Will it be ultimate, of a lasting nature? Will the idealistic dreamland never come back again? It is impossible to say.

However it be, the consequence of this realistic mentality of ours is that abstract definitions of God, transcendent doctrines which have the Christ for their object, discussions on the origin of evil, are no longer, even in the case of a believer most profoundly wedded to tradition, in the foreground of his preoccupations. He would rather not discuss them. He takes for granted that the doctrinal formulas which have been established in the past remain intangible. He considers that there are more pressing problems, because more concrete and positive. It is these, the moral, psychological and social questions which are being asked nowadays, that interest human life, its organisation and destiny. What is a Christian to think of them? What should be the attitude of the believer confronted with the various solutions offered? Which are the solutions that are in accord with his faith? What are the applications implied by the Gospel of Jesus? No longer has the believer to reconcile his Christian convictions with a philosophy or a science, but with human life itself. At bottom, the problem is the same, though it is considered in another aspect. It is to the honour of Origen that he was the first to seek, with indefatigable ardour, the solution of the problem as it offered itself in his day.

THE CHARACTER OF ORIGEN'S WRITINGS

HIS THOUGHT AND METHOD

THE CHARACTER OF ORIGEN'S WRITINGS

HIS THOUGHT AND METHOD

THE better to place Origen in time and space, we will first give a rapid sketch of his literary work. He was a voluminous writer, though only about a third of what he actually produced has come down to us. Part of this has been preserved in the original Greek: his *Contra Celsum*, the homilies on Jeremiah, the short treatises on prayer and martyrdom, a portion of the commentaries on John and on Matthew. Fragments and even whole pages of lost writings have come down to us in the *Florilegi* and the *Catenae*. Of recent years, these isolated fragments have been the object of interesting critical studies. They appear to be of less documentary importance than was supposed. The *Philocalia* of Basil and of Gregory contains important extracts from the *De Principiis* and from certain lost commentaries.

We are indebted to Rufinus of Aquileia and to Saint Jerome for the translation into Latin of a considerable number of homilies. Rufinus has left us a version of the *De Principiis*. Serious criticism has proved, with growing evidence, that these Latin versions are not to be trusted. The translators were afraid of offending their readers in the West if they retained in their text certain bold statements of Origen. There were fewer of these in the homilies than in the commentaries, though even the former astonished Jerome and Rufinus. Speaking generally, they modified the original text. It frequently happened that they either translated only a part of the original, or intercalated mitigating phrases. Jerome was fond of enhancing the somewhat colourless style of Origen with a few literary embellishments. In short, the translators of the fourth century showed not the slightest scruples in treating the text with the utmost freedom.

As the *De Principiis* is one of our main sources of information regarding the thought of Origen, we must state our opinion as to the real value and importance of the version left by Rufinus of Aquileia. No one denies that he took great liberties with the text he translated. Fortunately the Emperor Justinian, in his letter to the patriarch Mennas on the subject of Origen, inserted numerous quotations, more particularly from the first two books of the *De Principiis*. We are also aware that Jerome, for the purpose

ORIGEN'S WRITINGS

of demonstrating that Rufinus was untrustworthy, had given an exact translation of the same text. In his letter to Avitus, Bishop of Arles, he quotes several passages from it. We need only compare the quotations of Justinian and the extracts from Jerome's translation with the version of Rufinus to see that the latter is anything but faithful. True, this very year (1925), Bardy contests the value of these quotations and extracts in an excellent thesis, and attempts to save the reputation of Rufinus as a translator. A generous task, though one that does not seem likely to attain the object aimed at by the author. The critical conclusions of Koetschau, the latest editor of the *De Principiis*, seem to be well grounded. In our opinion, they might be made even stronger. Not only has Rufinus, in his translation, knowingly distorted the original, for the purpose of eliminating all that was too audacious in the doctrine, but very often he clearly does not understand the author's meaning. Origen sometimes expresses or indulges in reasonings which can be fully explained only if related to the time and circumstances in which he wrote them. Rufinus belongs to a period when the Church has held sovereign sway for a century; the mental atmosphere has profoundly changed. He is Latin and belongs to the West; Origen is

Greek and belongs to the East. To understand his author, the translator would have had to transfer himself to a time more than a century and a half gone by. This explains why, even in passages which have nothing to do with doctrine, Rufinus so often failed to catch the thought of Origen, with all its shades of meaning. Hence we can make use of the *De Principiis* only by checking its statements with texts taken from the author's Greek writings.

These remarks are necessary so that my hearers may be fully aware that the exposition we are about to make is based on documents which have passed through every critical test.

Before outlining the principal doctrines of our author, let us examine the nature of his mind. What is its dominating feature? As a theologian, is he an exegete or a dogmatist?

At first sight, the question appears strange and paradoxical. Did he not spend his life in studying and explaining the Scriptures? His first concern was to set up proof of the authentic text of the Greek Bible. His commentaries embraced almost the totality of the Christian Bible; his homilies are Bible studies. Even in his doctrinal writings, such as the *De Principiis*, numerous exegeses are to be found. He was— and aimed at being—quite exclusively an interpreter of the Bible and the apostolic tradition.

All the same, this is appearance rather than reality. Origen is essentially a Christian thinker or dogmatist; many are the reasons on which this opinion is founded.[1] We will dwell upon one only. This great commentator of the Bible writings never troubled himself to discover and emphasise the thought of the sacred author, his real feelings or particular opinions. This is what constitutes that which he himself calls the "historical meaning" of the text. As a rule, he is content to hint at it. Sometimes he does not even mention it; for the most part he treats it with a certain amount of scorn. Never does he neglect an opportunity to prove that, in some particular case, this meaning contradicts other parts of Scripture, or that it is unlikely to be true, and occasionally absurd. He is eager to attach blame to those who dwell upon this historical meaning; these are they who worship the letter. They have not yet advanced beyond the Jewish exegesis. What, then, is it that he seeks in the Bible text? His own theology, his own religious thought. Thanks to the method he has adopted of interpreting the ancient texts, he discovers in the Holy Book his own teaching on God and providence, his Christological doctrine, his doc-

[1] See our study in the *Revue d'Histoire et de Philosophie religieuse*, March–April, 1923.

trine on the origin and end of the Cosmos, on sin and redemption; in short, an entire system of " dogmas " of which the sacred authors never dreamt.

In effect, the Scriptures serve him admirably for illustrating his theology, while providing him with the divine authority which he cannot ignore. It must be recognised that Origen is a Christian philosopher who imagines he is explaining the Scriptures, whereas he is really exploiting them on behalf of his own dogmatic teaching. His commentaries tell us something of his theology, but nothing of the religion of Israel, nothing of the character or function of prophecy.

Since his writings are quite exclusively the documents of his thought, we will try to discover from them how this Christian philosopher and thinker conceives of the ensemble of things. What is his understanding of the Universe, to use a very convenient German expression, his *Weltanschauung*?

Confronted with the visible Cosmos, what are the questions he does not—and those that he does—ask?

Nowhere do we find that Origen seeks a rational and scientific explanation of the Universe. At no time does he ask himself, as did the physicists of old, of what elements the Universe is

ORIGEN'S WRITINGS 39

formed, how it is constructed, what are the laws that govern it, the relations of its parts to one another, whence come the beings that appear on it, what is the explanation of natural phenomena. All such problems he ignores. It is superfluous to add that, in his investigations relative to the Cosmos, it never enters into his mind to observe facts. He concerns himself in no way to acquire a precise and exact knowledge of phenomena. His knowledge of the Universe is as alien from our own as it can possibly be.

What then are the questions which the Cosmos suggests to him? Origen enquires into the rationale of the visible world and the cause of its appearance. What he wants is a metaphysical—even a moral—explanation. If God created it, what was the reason for doing so? What could be his object, his intention? Everybody is agreed that the Cosmos has a soul. What is the nature of this soul? The matter and the bodies that compose the Cosmos are very diverse, some more ethereal, others more opaque. What, then, is the explanation of this diversity? Finally, what is to be the destiny of this Cosmos? Is it to endure? If it has had a beginning, will it have an end? How will it perish? Could it by any possibility reappear? Is there any moral reason for its re-existence? Will this be in another form?

Will it be another Cosmos? If there is a plurality of worlds, will they succeed one another? Thus to Origen, the enigma of the world is not *what* it is, but *why* it is.

Here we may remark, in parenthesis, that the questions raised by Origen are bound to fill modern minds with amazement. Not for a moment can we imagine the possibility of anyone asking them. They appear futile to us, since we do not possess the means of answering them. However extensive our investigation of cosmic phenomena, it will never reveal the moral and metaphysical rationale of the Cosmos, on the supposition that there be one. Nevertheless, such questions as these are perfectly natural, even legitimate. Suppose a time comes when we finally attain to a rational and scientific explanation of our Cosmos, at least within the limits afforded by the study of phenomena. At that moment, will not thought logically be led to enquire what indeed can be the goal of this Universe whose structure, mechanism, and evolution it has finally come to understand? What is its destiny, its purpose? Can it really exist by virtue of some grandiose plan which we now have to discover? We might even ask whether there is not an intelligence, a will, behind this Cosmos and its phenomena. It may be that the intuitions of great religious souls

ORIGEN'S WRITINGS

have had faint glimmerings of these things. This is a question which science has neglected and put aside, but one which would again come before the mind, though under very different conditions, once science had completed its task. It seems as though the time will come when it will be difficult to prevent the intellect from seeking the solution of such a problem. The only reproach that one is justified in bringing against Origen is that he asked the question prematurely and attempted to solve the problem with inadequate means of information.

Origen, however, sees not only the visible world; he has the vision of an invisible and supra-sensible world in some way super-imposed upon the other. Nothing could be more logical. No sooner does he seek outside and above the visible Cosmos for the reason of its existence, its duration and its destiny, than he is compelled to postulate a transcendent world. In default of logic, the example of Plato and other philosophers appears to have suggested to him the conception of the metaphysical Cosmos. At once his imagination peoples it with innumerable entities and heavenly beings. Origen conceives of this invisible Cosmos as more real and positive than the visible Cosmos. He entertains no doubt as to the superiority of the ideal world. We shall return to this point subsequently.

Such in its main lines is Origen's conception of the totality of things. To forget or be unaware of this is to be convicted of a complete misunderstanding of his thought. The significance of the most characteristic pages of his *De Principiis* and of his commentary on John would escape the reader; nothing would be more irksome, less vital and luminous. Placing ourselves at the author's standpoint, everything is clear and vivid. The exposition here given is an indispensable preface to the study of his theology.

This conception is fundamentally speculative and metaphysical, the product exclusively of a powerful imagination guided by a bold and intrepid dialectic. It would be impossible to conceive of anything farther removed from our own mental habits. To understand it, we must do all we can to carry ourselves back to a time when the majority of the philosophers contemporary with Origen had the same mentality as himself.

Before expounding the main doctrines of our theologian, it remains for us to examine his method of thought. And here, too, we must not allow ourselves to be deceived by appearances. When we first read him, we obtain the impression that allegory is the method he employs, for it is to be found everywhere in his writings. He

ORIGEN'S WRITINGS

would appear to build up his ideas by allegorical processes.

But how could this be? What is allegory as it was then practised, as it was applied by Philo of Alexandria, by Plutarch, by Origen himself? It is the art of discovering in a text an idea which the author seems to have had, but which is not apparent in the literal meaning of this text. The author has concealed it beneath words that have a meaning which is not that of the idea. And yet, on close examination, the text contains some word which indicates the essential idea of the writer. This word is the sign (σημεῖον), so to speak, of its presence. It is for the interpreter to be sufficiently keen to perceive it. Once he is on the track and suspects the real meaning of the text, he need only compare with other passages the one he is studying. Light will flash forth, and suddenly the essence of the sacred writer's idea will appear in all its luminous clarity. We shall then hold the key of the enigma which lay hidden beneath some simple commonplace meaning. If such is allegory, it is evident that the interpreter finds in it the transcendent idea he attributes to his text only because he has put it there. Unless he had it already in his mind, he would not discover it. When he thinks he discerns it in the text, he is the dupe of his own method of interpretation. As a matter of fact, he reads his own thought into it. Thus does Origen transform the Old Testament into a sort of illustration of his religious philosophy.

If this is so, it is not the allegorical method which suggests his ideas, it neither forms his thought nor governs its development and evolution. It simply confirms and strengthens his ideas. He is all the more wedded to them because he thinks he had discovered them in an ancient sacred text.

The question we have just asked still remains unanswered. We do not yet know what rule governed the thought and reason of Origen. As might have been expected, it is philosophy that gives to him, and to every thinking man of his age, the rule and method of his thinking processes. This method is the dialectic created by Socrates and the Sophists, elaborated and fashioned into a marvellous instrument of speculation and argumentation by Plato, Aristotle and the Stoics. Along with many other instances of this, we may find a striking one in the opening paragraphs of the third book of the *De Principiis*. Origen wishes to demonstrate free-will. He starts with the idea of movement which he defines, reaching, by successive eliminations, the one essential feature, freedom of choice. The reasoning is carried on according to the strictest

ORIGEN'S WRITINGS

rules of Aristotelian dialectic. Moreover, where except among philosophers could our theologian have expected to find a method of thought and demonstration? Assuredly he would not have acquired one from prophetism or ancient Hebraism. The rabbis might have taught him an infinitely subtle method of reasoning, if he had been acquainted with their theology. This, however, Philo of Alexandria held in disdain, preferring the method of the Greeks. Indeed, one could not in those days claim to appeal to the intellectuals, unless one carried on the discussion by the rules everywhere accepted in the schools.

What then is the allegorical method, according to Origen? It is a complementary method. He has to discover his teachings in the Scriptures. Allegory is the learned and well-established means, both scientific and philosophical, of discerning a philosophy or a theology in writings, ancient and revered as oracular, and so Origen uses it because he needs it. He is acquainted with its subtlest processes and excels in applying them with a skill which never fails him. And so, in the commentaries as well as in the *De Principiis*, when he wishes to prove some teaching or other, he gives us a dual demonstration. The one is purely dialectical; in reality, the essential one. The other is exegetical and scriptural, bringing to rational argumentation the testimony of divinity, the seal and guarantee of the divinely inspired document. The order of both kinds of demonstration is of no importance whatsoever: now it is by the one, now by the other, that Origen begins to expound the proof of his doctrine. Thus, allegory does not give him his ideas and doctrines, it is—and can only be—of use in vouching for them.

If Origen is really a religious philosopher far more than an interpreter of the Scriptures, and after all uses them only to illustrate his ideas, one wonders if it was really necessary to retain the said Scriptures. On this point certain Gnostic theologians were more radical than himself. Marcion rejects the Old Testament which, to his mind, is no more than a Jewish book. Ptolemy repudiates much of it which does not find favour with his searching criticism. The *Pistis Sophia* retains the penitential Psalms, but what does it do with the rest? Origen keeps the entire Bible; he spends his life in commenting on it, aiming to be simply an exegete and declaring it to be divinely inspired. In his eyes it is a sort of collection of divine oracles.

In his passionate attachment to the old book he proves himself a true child of his age. In the second and third centuries, every great philosophy and important religious doctrine makes appeal to the past for its credentials, the warrant of its truth. This is an outstanding fact in the history of Greek ideas, which can be explained only by the evolution of philosophic thought in the three or four centuries preceding the time of Origen. In the days of the great classic philosophies, from Socrates to Chrysippus, thought has absolute confidence in itself. With the audacity of youth, it flings itself into dialectic, believing reason to be infallible. The piercing criticism of the New Academy, of Arcesilas and Carneades, shatters this confidence. The scepticism first of Pyrrho, and more particularly of Aenesidemus and Sextus, finally dissipates the early illusion and shows us dialectic committing suicide and indeed drying up the very springs of thought.

What then does philosophy do? Will it give up living, condemn itself to cease thinking? Impossible. No longer finding within itself the warrant of its doctrines, it seeks without. It appeals to the past, to the ancient wisdom, to old myths and the most revered writings.

In the first century of the Christian era, certain names receive a sort of new consecration. Thus, an entirely new school claims authority from Pythagoras. As his doctrines are unknown, apart from a few elements preserved by tradition, he is credited with a philosophy which belongs far more to Plato and the Stoics, and is himself transformed into a legendary character. Plato becomes a demi-god. Dion Prusaensis regards Heracles as the ideally perfect philosopher, whereas for Epictetus and the Cynics it is Diogenes who is the model. Never before had the superstition of certain names been carried to such extremes. A like veneration was bestowed on certain old books. Maximus Tyrius quotes Homer as others quote the Bible. If we are to believe many a philosopher, the whole of truth is to be found in the Iliad and the Odyssey. Remembering what Plato says regarding the wisdom of the priests of Egypt, Plutarch makes his own the old myth of Isis and Osiris, finding therein, by a subtle interpretation, the whole of his philosophy. The Jews of Alexandria feel the need of invoking antiquity in favour of the doctrines. Philo regards Moses as the philosopher of his dreams. The Gnostics themselves occasionally followed the same tendency. Whereas Marcion is determined to know only the Gospels and Paul's Epistles, duly cleansed of their Judaical leaven, the Gnostics of the *Philosophumena* of Hippolytus, along with those of the Coptic

ORIGEN'S WRITINGS

documents, rely on the most incongruous traditions and writings. All of these are good, provided only they be ancient. The sects that have secret books and esoteric traditions are incalculable in number.

In regarding the Bible as a collection of oracles and declaring it to be divinely inspired, Origen is actuated by like motives. He needs something which he can claim as the oldest authority; it must be possible for him to interpret the Scriptures in such fashion as to find his doctrines in them. This is why the allegorical meaning is the only one he takes into account. If the literal sense of the Bible is upheld, he cannot possibly read his theology into it. His scorn of the literal sense of the text knows no bounds. As a rule, it is only for conscience sake that he mentions it. He is quite aware that he cannot ignore it altogether, but he is not sparing in his criticisms of it. He is continually proving either that this meaning contradicts other passages of the Scriptures, or that it is improbable, even absurd, or—a thing far more serious in his eyes—that it implies a notion of God and His providence, which is unworthy of Him and might justly be regarded as impious. In the second chapter of the first book of *De Principiis*, he goes even further, showing that it is because the Jews rely on the literal meaning of the

Messianic passages in the Old Testament that they refuse to believe in Christ. The reason why Marcion and his school contrast the God of the Old Testament with the God of Jesus Christ, is because they interpret literally the Scripture texts which represent God as being jealous and vindictive, fond of war, and the author of all evils. In short, simple-minded believers, he says, do not differentiate between the God of Moses and the Prophets, and the Heavenly Father of the Gospels; but as they also give a literal interpretation to the passages which offend Marcion, the outcome is that they attribute to God feelings which could be none other than those that animate the most cruel and inhuman of mankind. Even in his homilies, also, Origen incessantly asserts the allegorical meaning of the Scriptures. On this point, he would like to complete the education of his hearers and initiate them into the right understanding of the Bible.

We may then ask what becomes of the Holy Bible itself, if Origen's method be employed. Allegory will completely transform it; beautiful and edifying sentences may still be found, but nothing remains of its real substance. The allegorist ignores such things as a primitive Hebrew religion, a national Jehovah, prophetism, the piety of the psalmists. He is unable to

ORIGEN'S WRITINGS

come under their influence. Accordingly, it is not surprising that Origen is in no way indebted to the Old Testament, as the Old Testament owes nothing to his exegesis.

What does he owe to the New Testament *qua* sacred book? In his polemic against Celsus, Origen vigorously defends the material facts of the Gospel story. He does not allow them to vanish into thin air by a learned interpretation of them. All the same, the "tomes" of his commentary on Matthew that have come down to us show that he applied his allegorical exegesis to the Gospel, to the sayings and parables of Jesus. The result is that the true meaning of the passages he allegorises has eluded him. It cannot be affirmed that primitive evangelism—any more than Paulinism—was well understood by our theologian, and the direct influence upon Origen of the writings of the New Testament was after all only partial.

What, then, is the source of his faith? More than all else, it is living tradition (ἡ παράδοσις). It is no more primitive evangelism than it is Paulinism that passed from mouth to mouth. It is this entirely oral Christianity, the writings of which—scarcely yet canonical—were but a reflection, which many regarded as too pallid, that had won over his father Leonides and inspired him with heroic faith. It is this oral

Christianity, far more than books, which inspired the youthful Origen. And so, when he begins to write his *De Principiis*, he claims that he is—and aims at being—nothing but the interpreter of the Apostolic tradition.

THE DOCTRINE OF GOD

THE DOCTRINE OF GOD

WHAT are the essential characteristics of our theologian's doctrine of God? First of all, transcendence. The God he conceives is more abstract than the God of Plato himself. Many are the texts in Origen's works that insist on the absolute spirituality of God. For instance, in the commentary on John (chap. XIII, verses 21-25), referring to the phrase: God is spirit; in the *De Principiis*, chap. I, a passage which reproduces the same argumentation and the same Scripture texts; in the *De Oratione*, XXIII, 1-5, with reference to the expression in the Lord's Prayer: "Who art in heaven";—in all these texts he vigorously rejects the idea that God possesses a body. Far from attributing to Him a corporeal nature, however slight, he asserts that God is pure invisible incorporeal intelligence. Both reason and Scripture agree in conceiving of Him under this aspect. Clearly Origen is seeking after terms which will best express absolute transcendence in order to apply them to God. He is not only alone (μόνος) He is unique (ἕνας) (*De Princ.*, I, 1, 6). He is being *per se* (οὐσια). He even goes so far as to declare that God is not only above the All, but even beyond being *per se*. He is αὐτοθεος. He is above wisdom, truth, eternal life (*In Joh.*, II, 23; XIII, 3). As we see, Origen is more of a Platonist than Plato himself. When Celsus, under the pretext that Christians call God spirit, accuses them of having adopted the Stoic doctrine of the immanence of God, he indignantly protests. For the same reason, he is unable to accept the anthropomorphisms of the Old Testament, which he looks upon as unworthy of God. By means of allegory, he eliminates them whenever he finds them in a text of Scripture. The fact is that Origen, like many another philosopher of his day, considers that if there is introduced into God even the slightest particle of matter, He will be relegated to the domain of the multiple, the mortal, the perishable. This thought he expresses in the following passage of his *De Oratione* (chap. XXIII, 3): "It is my object to annihilate a paltry conception of God: that of those people who regard God as localised in heaven. I will not permit it to be said that God sojourns in a material place. You might as well say that He Himself is corporeal. This would result in the most impious doctrines. One would suppose that He is divisible, material,

THE DOCTRINE OF GOD

and perishable. Now these are the properties of bodies".

On the other hand, this God whom Origen conceives as all that is most transcendent and abstract, is pre-eminently the Living One. This he asserts in very remarkable terms in his commentary on John (II, 17 and 18). "Absolute life", he says, "is found in God alone. No being, not even Christ, possesses unchangeable life, pure immortality". This God is a person, for He is conscious of Himself. He contemplates Himself, and is absorbed in self-knowledge; He rejoices with unspeakable joy, for He finds within Himself the source of His contentment (*In Joh.*, XXXII, 28). *Qua* personality, this God has moral qualities; He unites within Himself more particularly justice and goodness. This is stoutly maintained by Origen against Marcion and his school (*De Princ.*, II, 5, 3). His God is even goodness absolute. "He is good *per se*", "He is genuinely good". He is αὐτοαγαθὸς. In Jesus Christ himself, goodness does not possess this absolute character. Take the term in the moral sense rather than in the metaphysical one which Plato gave to it (χρηστότης rather than ἀγαθότης); we see that such a God cannot be conceived as the author, in whatsoever degree, either of moral evil or of evil in general.

This dual nature of the God of Origen is

manifested in His relations with beings and with the Cosmos. On the one hand, He eludes thought; He is inapprehensible. On the other hand, although He does not enter into contact with flesh and matter, and acts only from a distance, He yet makes His presence felt. If God is not immanent in the world, Deity is. It is by this that He exerts a very effective providence. As He is good in essence, He acts only in order to obtain the amelioration of the sinner. Never does He punish for the sake of punishing; the affliction He imposes is essentially educational; it excludes the very idea of expiation.

Can these two aspects of God, as Origen conceives Him, be reconciled? Do they not appear to exclude each other? Nowhere does our theologian ask this question. He does not seem to perceive that his doctrine involves a somewhat apparent contradiction.

We will now consider a third characteristic of the God of Origen, one scarcely less important than the preceding: that God is limited. Perhaps fidelity to the thought of our author would compel us to say that God has imposed certain limitations upon Himself. He is limited by His very nature; He cannot do that which is unjust and evil. "When we say that all is possible to God, we know that this does not mean what does not exist and cannot be thought. We likewise say that God cannot do what is morally evil; this would be saying that God can make Himself cease being God. Indeed, if God does what is evil, He is no longer God" (*C. Celsum*, V, 23). In a fragment which Justinian gives from his letter to Mennas, we read: "It must be asserted that the power of God has bounds. We ought not, under the pretence of respect, to do away with the limits of His power. For if this power were limitless, necessarily it would be unaware of itself. It is in the nature of the limitless to be inapprehensible. God therefore created all that He could reach, embrace and subject to His providence" (*De Princ.*, II, 9, 1 Ed. Koetschau, p. 164).

Then what is the source of this doctrine? Is it of Biblical origin? From what we have already seen, it is not likely to have borrowed anything whatsoever from the Old Testament. Origen so distinctly repudiates the Jehovah of the historical books that he is certain he has retained nothing of Him. Does the God of the Prophets, an absolute monarch, project His image on Origen's conception of God? Is not a God Who is exclusively the judge and justiciary of Judaism supremely antipathetic to our theologian? All that can be said is that the Old Testament strengthened his monotheism, but in no way contributed to form his idea of God.

How far is his doctrine indebted to the New Testament, more particularly to the Gospels? Assuredly he allegorised it to a considerable extent, though he did not go to the same extremes as with the Old Testament. He retains the essence of the material facts, and even of the words of the Gospel. Did he really understand Jesus and his message? This may be doubted. Nevertheless, like Marcion and others, he felt that goodness was the essential feature of the God of Jesus Christ. While unwilling to separate it from the righteousness or justice of God, he was deeply conscious of this goodness, whereas others, like Tertullian, quite overlooked it.

Of all the influences which contributed to form his doctrine of God, the most apparent—and at the same time the most profound—was Plato and Platonism. It was Plato who inculcated in him that transcendence which he regards as an essential character of God. The connection is so clear that there is no need to dwell on it. And it was Plato who revealed to him the moral aspect of God and of His providence. In proclaiming God as the framer of souls, he shows himself the true child of the great philosopher. Like many another, he pondered long on the end of the second book of the *Republic* and on the tenth book of the *Laws*. He fully understood

THE DOCTRINE OF GOD

why Plato exiled Homer from his city-state. He is aware that this was because the poet sets forth an idea of Deity that is unworthy, one which the philosopher cannot tolerate. It is in Plato that he has read the following sentences which have graven themselves upon his mind: "God is the cause of all good and never of evil", and again: "It is impious to maintain that God is responsible for evil". Chapter nine of the tenth book of the *Laws* certainly made a deep impression upon him, for it is here that Plato expounds his conception of providence. According to him, providence is exclusively educational, an idea which Origen is constantly to reproduce.

It is scarcely possible to exaggerate the influence exercised by the religious ideas of Plato, notably during the second century. Perhaps there is no philosopher—with the exception of the Epicureans and a few contemporary Sceptics—who does not formulate with greater or less preciseness the doctrines of the author of the *Republic* and the *Laws* regarding God and providence. From this time forward, there are affirmations which no philosopher would any longer permit himself. Plutarch is a striking instance of the fact to which we refer. The ideas he expressed in his *De sera numinis vindicta* are simply the development of those of Plato.

The philosopher of Chaeroneia is imbued with the doctrine of an educational providence which seeks after the good and the amelioration of human beings. On this point, there is no difference whatsoever between Plutarch and Origen. Unwittingly they meet in Plato, coming under the sovereign influence of his religious thought.

Nevertheless, although Origen certainly read and reflected on Plato himself, it was partially at least through the Platonism of his time that he understood him. All the disciples—acknowledged or unacknowledged—of Plato in the second and third centuries show a marked tendency to carry the transcendence of God farther than even Plato had done. The Neo-Pythagoreans of Alexandria teach that "God is above all thought and all being". Philo of Alexandria, about the same time, says that "God is superior to virtue, to good *per se*". All the Gnostic theologians, who follow Plato more or less, express themselves in the same terms. To Valentinus, to Basilides and to Ptolemy, God is above and beyond the world of ideas, of essences, of aeons. He is wholly lost in abstraction, to such an extent that the problem which concerns these theologians is to imagine an externalisation of God—or rather of Deity regarded as detached from God Himself—

THE DOCTRINE OF GOD

which would bring it into contact with beings. And lastly, Plotinus also relegated God to a sort of hypertranscendence. As we have seen, this tendency is very marked in Origen; there can be no doubt but that, on this point, he is a Platonist of his age.

Is the effect of Stoicism upon Origen much less marked than that of Platonism? The Porch regards God as immanent in the Cosmos. He is its principle of life and movement. Zeno is poles asunder from Plato. From this point of view it may be said that, whereas Platonic transcendence went farther away from Hellenism, Stoicism drew nearer to it. The ancient Greeks set up a state of familiarity between gods and men. Stoicism considers that God is in us and we are in God. The very serious drawback implied in this immanence postulated by Stoicism is that of materialising God. He was interchangeable with the Cosmos. Hence He risked a diminution of self, defilement through contact with matter. This is the very danger so strongly felt by Plato. All Platonists are well aware of it, and are anxious to remove the danger; Origen is no exception. On the other hand, his doctrine of the immanence of God ensured indisputable superiority for Stoicism. Through it he rendered God more of an object of sense, more actual and vital to man. The Stoic, if he was religious, felt God quite close to him. However philosophical its expression, his piety became more intimate and more vibrant.

In a letter he wrote to Lucilius, Seneca exhorts him not to seek God outside of himself in the distant heavens, but within himself. *Prope est a te Deus; tecum est, intus est.* Marcus Aurelius also expresses himself in like terms; probably this latter philosopher in particular interprets God strictly in the Stoic sense. The interior God of the great emperor is the law and divine principle of the Cosmos, not a person. In no way does this God inspire in him a mystic piety, the cult he offers Him is purely rational. This is not so with Epictetus; the feeling caused in him by God or Zeus is far from being strictly philosophical. He speaks of Him with a degree of emotion which no one could feel for an abstraction, for an impersonal law. The God of Epictetus is a person whom the Stoic sage does not define and never discusses, but who is very living in his eyes. He regards himself as His messenger; it is God Who has set him at the post where he finds himself; he has no right to desert this post, but must wait until Zeus releases him. The admirable passage in which he speaks of this is well known (*Discourses*, I, 16): "Since most of you have become blind, ought there not to be some man

THE DOCTRINE OF GOD

to fill this office, and on behalf of all to sing the hymn to God? For what else can I do, a lame old man, than sing hymns to God? If then I was a nightingale, I would do the part of a nightingale, if I were a swan, I would do like a swan. But now I am a rational creature, and I ought to praise God, this is my work; I do it, nor will I desert this post, so long as I am allowed to keep it; and I exhort you to join in this same song ". No philosopher of antiquity, not even Socrates or Plato, has sounded forth so clear and definite a note of pure mysticism.

Origen, like Clement his master, was profoundly influenced by Stoicism. He employs its philosophical terminology, as we may see from the first few paragraphs of the third book of the *De Principiis*. He also borrowed from it his psychological analyses and the essential part of his cosmology. For him as for the Stoics the Cosmos is a gigantic animal, a ζῶον. It thus appears likely that he acquired from these philosophers, to a considerable extent, that sense of the divine life and of the actual and perceptible influence of God which seems to us so slightly reconcilable with that extreme transcendence which he attributes to this same God.

Have we exhausted the elements which, as a whole, formed Origen's idea of God? We do not think so. As a matter of fact, in the feeling inspired in him by the God in Whom he believes, there is more than the consciousness of a contact, more than simple intimacy after the fashion of Epictetus; there is a very strong aspiration after mysticism. He dreams of rising to God, of contemplating Him and one day living in Him. The attraction he experiences is a singularly ardent one. Judging by what remains of his commentary and homilies on *Solomon's Song*, in the versions of Rufinus and Jerome, he has expressed this mysticism with incredible fervour. While Origen surpassed other commentators in his commentaries, he surpassed himself in his commentary on the *Song*. It may be that the mysticism of our theologian is essentially intellectual. He aspires to behold in God the prototypes of things, eternal ideas, and for him supreme felicity manifestly consists in finally attaining to the solution of the problems that beset him. The *Phaedrus* of Plato set its stamp on the mysticism of Origen. None the less true is it that while the form of his mysticism is more Platonic than Christian, its substance is essentially Christian. The feeling that inspires and gives it life draws its strength from the common faith of believers. Of course, we would not dream of denying that there has existed a mysticism which is not Christian; Plotinus, and Philo of Alexandria before him, are authentic mystics. The very great mystics, however, have always been Christian, and they appeared in the earliest days of Christianity. They form a venerable procession beginning with Saint Paul and the author of the fourth Gospel, continuing with Ignatius of Antioch, Origen, Saint Augustine, Saint Bernard and the great mystics of the Middle Ages, the author of the *Imitation* and the great Christians of modern times. Mysticism is indeed a Christian reality; in the last analysis it constitutes the main element in our author's doctrine of God. However composite it be, this doctrine is profoundly homogeneous and vital. Its various constituents are blended in an ardent conviction which Origen proclaims on every occasion. It inspires his thought, fashions his exegesis and gives its own special character to his piety. To apprehend its originality to the full, it was necessary to find its source and origin, alike intellectual and emotional.

We see what emphasises the distinctive nature of the doctrine of Origen when we consider the doctrines which he combated. First, there is that of Marcion and his school; he never loses an opportunity of denouncing it, and even in his homilies he does not spare the heresiarch. Marcion, greatly struck by the contrast which Saint Paul makes between Law and Faith,

Judaism and Christianity, had gone so far as to contrast the God of the Old Testament with the God of Jesus Christ. The former, maker of heaven and earth, was the God of the Jews. In the historical books and in the Prophets, Marcion points out all those traits which seemed incompatible with the character of the Heavenly Father. He was cruel and fond of war, vindictive and jealous; His only good quality was justice. He was just after the fashion of an inexorable judge. The saints of the Old Testament were His servants. Now, He was not the one supreme God. This God was unknown to mankind. He was alien to the world since He had not created it and did not rule it by His providence. Suddenly, in the fifteenth year of the reign of Tiberius, Jesus appeared, revealing to the world the true God. The latter is essentially good, and desires the redemption of men.

Tertullian, consummate dialectitian as he was, combated this relative ditheism, since the two gods of Marcion are by no means on an equality. He proved the contradictory nature of the Marcionite conception. In a totally different way does Origen combat Marcion. First of all, he refutes him on the ground of exegesis. The opposition which he thinks he finds between certain declarations of the Old Testament relating to God and those of Jesus Christ, is non-

THE DOCTRINE OF GOD

existent. Marcion has made the mistake of taking these declarations literally. They have another meaning, which a sane exegesis reveals. And so, thanks to an allegorical interpretation, our theologian effaces the contrast which appeared to justify the doctrine of the heresiarch. In his *De Principiis* (I, 10) Origen undertakes to prove that justice and goodness cannot thus be separated in God; on the contrary, the one requires the other. In this passage, he gives proof of the admirable accuracy of his psychological acumen. He saw that without justice there is no true goodness; just as, without goodness, there is no true justice.

All the same, he was not so far removed from the heretic as he imagined. He, too, was aware of the very real difference between the Jehovah of the Old Testament and the Heavenly Father of Jesus Christ. He does not acknowledge, any more than does Marcion, that the true God of the Christians can be jealous and vindictive, cruel and bellicose. To claim that such is the character of God seems to him as impious—even blasphemous—as to maintain that God has a human form, with eyes, arms and feet. Both his feelings as a Christian and his preoccupations as a Platonist reject the conception of God which Marcion criticises. If he does not go so far as to postulate the two gods of this latter, it is not from lack of logic, but rather because allegory offers him a wonderful instrument for overcoming the difficulty. One can well understand why he is so resolutely attached to this method.

With like severity Origen criticises the idea of God commonly held by the majority of Christians. It must be acknowledged that there was the greatest confusion of ideas amongst them on this point. For our information we have the writings of the Apostolic Fathers, writings that were eminently popular. All Christians are unanimous in proclaiming that there is but one God. This did not prevent them from admitting that, apart from the one true God, there might be inferior deities or divine beings: the daimons, for instance. But while they were all agreed in believing in only one God, maker of heaven and earth, they were not united as to what must be thought of His nature and character. Some wondered if He had a body; others denied this. Some saw in Him the supreme Judge Who rewards or punishes every man according to his deserts; others considered Him to be a veritable despot, harsh and arbitrary. Men like Ignatius of Antioch had such a feeling of mystic piety for Jesus Christ that they made scarcely any distinction between him and God Himself. It was

THE DOCTRINE OF GOD

principally on the question of God's providence that there was the greatest confusion of ideas. On the whole, God was made responsible for all that happens on earth. He is the author of evil as well as of good, of misfortune and of happiness alike. Persecution and catastrophe come about because He has willed it so.[1]

Origen attempts persistently to correct this extremely simple and imperfect idea. He thinks it arises from the literal interpretation of the Scriptures: a fact which he brings up as a grievance against simple-minded believers. These fall into the same error as the Jews. Such believers Origen treats very severely, being almost as harsh with them as Tertullian was with those he called psychics. His homilies are a persevering attempt to raise them to a higher level. He would like to teach them to read the Scriptures intelligently. In other words, it is his endeavour to popularise allegorical interpretation, the one certain means, according to him, of rectifying their idea of God.

Origen was beset by a dread lest Biblical literalism should pervert the idea of God, and indeed this dread was justified. History was to prove our theologian right. In the seven-

---

[1] We have examined this point in detail in an article of the *Revue de l'Histoire des Religions*, January–February, 1911.

teenth century, the Puritans of England and the Covenanters of Scotland believed in the uniform inspiration of the Bible throughout; they made no difference between any page whatsoever of the Old Testament and the most sublime passages in the Gospels. Their theopneusty extended to the letter as well as to the spirit of the whole Bible. Doubtless influenced by the tragic circumstances of the times in which they lived, they became passionately attached to the God of Hosts of the Old Testament. His authority served to cast a veil of sombre fanaticism over all excesses. The letter kills, says the Apostle Paul, and but too frequently were their actions a sanguinary commentary on the expression.

Origen was deeply conscious that his sublime doctrine, which admirably blended and harmonised the purest Greek thought with the teaching of Jesus himself, could not co-exist by the side of a gross literalism which, he well knew, was fatal to what he believed the truth regarding God. The only way to safeguard this truth was to interpret the Old Testament in accordance with the rules of allegory. This has been understood and practised by all who have been his disciples.

In the long run, the allegorical method was bound to prove a failure. It had to show itself

THE DOCTRINE OF GOD

as what it actually was, artificial and calculated to obscure the meaning of the Biblical authors. To avoid the danger he perceived so clearly, it would have been necessary for Origen to live in modern times, to have been acquainted with the historical method. Then he would have recognised what a real difference there is between the Old Testament conception of God and that of Jesus Christ. He would even have seen that the idea of God differs in various portions of the Old Testament itself. That of the historical books is greatly inferior to that of the Prophets. That of the Decalogue is not in accord with that of Ezekiel, and the second Isaiah rises far superior to all other worshippers of Jehovah. He appears to have understood that these differences have not their origin, as Marcion thought, in God, Who is not the same God in the Gospels as in the Old Testament, but that they are the creation of men who, according to the age, have had a more or less pure and lofty idea of God. And so the Old Testament stood forth as the history of the evolution of the idea of God among the most religious of peoples.

No wonder that Origen neither anticipated the times and seasons nor read the future. He introduced into his doctrine of God the finest thought of the greatest of the philosophers of antiquity and the essence of that vision of the Father which Jesus revealed to the world. Alas, he failed to be understood! In the following chapter we shall try to explain the reasons for such an amazing lack of comprehension.

COSMOLOGY

COSMOLOGY

IT is not easy to discover precisely what are the views of Origen on the Universe, nor where he obtained his data. The sources of information are not all of equal value; certain are untrustworthy. He wrote a commentary on Genesis; only a fragment remains. This loss is greatly to be regretted, for he certainly expounded his views on the origin of the Cosmos when dealing with the early chapters of Genesis. There is a Latin version of his homilies on Genesis, but only one of these speaks of the Creation. It makes no mention whatsoever of the author's own views.

In the second book of the *De Principiis*, Origen states at considerable length his teachings on cosmology. This, however, is a part of the translation of Rufinus which calls for the greatest caution. Nothing could be more natural, seeing that the cosmological doctrine of Origen is the very one which diverges most widely from the ideas current amongst Christians. While translating him, Rufinus continually encountered views which he knew would prove intolerable to the orthodox of his time. The temptation to tone them down was very strong. That the greatest number of heresies was found in this part of Origen's book is proved by the fact that when the Emperor Justinian undertakes to bring to trial the great theologian, it is here that he finds the principal texts which he incriminates. When Jerome wished to prove that Rufinus had intentionally distorted the text of Origen in his version, it was from the second book of the *De Principiis* that he took most of his examples. How unwise therefore to trust unreservedly to Rufinus! His version can be utilised only after subjecting it to severe criticism, as Koetschau has done. We need but supplement—and perhaps emphasise—his conclusions, and then we may consider that we have a solid foundation upon which to expound the doctrine of Origen.

We have characterised in its ensemble Origen's idea of the Universe, both visible and invisible; now we must take it in detail and, more especially, see in what way it is related to Greek philosophy.

We regard cosmology as the science of the Universe, or at all events the rational and scientific explanation of our limited Cosmos. We wish to know how it was formed, the origin and constitution of our globe, how life appeared thereon, the birth and development of man.

COSMOLOGY

In olden days it was Aristotle who most brilliantly represented this point of view, collecting and classifying a multitude of observations and establishing the science of nature. Not being understood, he had no successors. Stoics and Epicureans indeed have a conception of the Cosmos, of its origin, its continuance and destiny, but this conception is an entirely hypothetical and metaphysical conception; it owes nothing to the observation of facts. Whether consciously or not, it is Plato who is followed. It would be impossible to exaggerate the influence of the *Timaeus* on all who thought and reflected, an influence which could be nothing less than fatal to any attempt at a scientific explanation of the Universe. The *Timaeus* accustomed the mind to regard the Cosmos entirely in a metaphysical aspect. Is it not a powerful attempt to prove that the Cosmos is the product of the spirit? Such is the outstanding concern of the author. The Cosmos is a reflection of the higher world, and it is there that we must look both for its rationale and for the secret of its destiny. In this conception, the facts and problems that it raises are thrust entirely into the background.

This is the point of view which henceforth asserts itself, and which we find in all philosophers. It is that of Philo of Alexandria, of

Plutarch and of Plotinus. And it is the only one known to Christian thinkers who, although in common with the philosophers they have an absolutely metaphysical conception of the Cosmos, have yet enriched it with an entirely new feature. Their conception is both moral and metaphysical, as is seen for the first time in the Gnostic theologians. This dual character is strongly marked in the speculation of a Valentinus who explains the appearance of the Cosmos by moral as well as by metaphysical reasons. The moral reasons are even predominant. But for the fall of Sophia, neither matter nor the Cosmos would have existed, seeing that the four elements were born of the passions of the fallen Aeon.

As we shall see, Origen also seeks in the transcendent world for the reason of existence of the Cosmos, and this reason is also more moral than metaphysical. It is the same with his conception of the suprasensible world.

It, too, springs direct from Platonism. We have already seen how great was the influence of Plato's religious ideas in the days of Clement and Origen. A large number of men looked upon certain pages of the *Laws* and the *Republic* as truly in the nature of a revelation. Those who were thus moved to enthusiasm could no longer think of God, the gods, providence,

COSMOLOGY

except through the mind of Plato. Even the sceptic Lucian came under the influence of the great philosopher. After Plato, there came into being decidedly old-fashioned ways of speaking about religion. No less profound was the influence of Plato's ideas regarding the suprasensible world. His genius conjures up an invisible domain superimposed on the visible world. Above the material Cosmos towers a transcendent world which Plato peoples with eternal Ideas, lauding its immaculate beauty in language of incomparable charm. There is the immortal description of the *Phaedrus*; the pages of the *Republic* in which he contrasts the domain of the immutable, of that which is *per se*, with the domain of becoming, of the relative and the perishable; there is the image of the Cave, the discourse of Diotima in the *Symposium* on the beauty of eternal Ideas; there are the innumerable passages wherein he celebrates the rapture of the spirit in contemplation on pure Ideas and the enthusiasm—his own word—which takes possession of him at the sight.

There can be no doubt but that such pictures were graven on the memories of all in the second and third centuries. After reading them again and again and meditating upon them, it was impossible to dispel the divine vision they summoned up. Henceforth the Platonic image of the suprasensible world became part of one's very nature. The Universe could no longer be conceived except as dual: the visible world, and the transcendent world towering above it. Origen, Christian though he was, came under the spell. He was one of the young intellectuals of his day who read Plato; he had too many secret affinities with the great philosopher not to be won over by him. His imagination is inflamed; his thoughts soar aloft. Justin Martyr says that the eternal Ideas of Plato gave him wings, as it were. So penetrating and far-reaching a genius as that of Origen could not remain indifferent to the Platonic visions. Under the influence of Plato he accustomed himself to believe that the transcendent world not only exists, but that it is more real than the material world. The latter perishes, the "intelligible world" can never die.

Like Philo of Alexandria, like Plotinus, Valentinus, and certain Gnostic masters of the *Philosophumena*, the imagination of Origen peoples with inhabitants the suprasensible world. As a rule he calls them entities or essences endowed with reason, οὐσίαι λογικαί, sometimes natures endowed with reason. In the original fragments of the *De Principiis*, he usually designates them as νόες, intelligences; he also uses the terms, forces or ideas: δυνάμεις or ἰδέαι. Certain

COSMOLOGY 83

of these appellations are Aristotelian, others Platonic; the terms δυνάμεις and λόγοι are Stoic. Thus it is originally from the three great philosophies that Origen borrowed the technical designations he applies to the inhabitants of the suprasensible world. The result is that to him they are not—as to a Platonist—pure abstractions; they are also beings or essences of beings, as Aristotle calls them, and living forces like those which Stoicism regards as immanent in the Cosmos.

These are exclusively philosophical entities, and yet Origen afterwards claims that he finds them in the Scriptures. Following the example of Philo of Alexandria who regarded the angels of the Old Testament as being in the same category as the Ideas and the "germinal reasons" of the philosophers, Origen identifies the abstractions, beings, spirits (πνεύματα in the Stoic sense) of his suprasensible world with certain entities mentioned in the Scriptures. For instance, Colossians i, 16 and Ephesians i, 21, he regarded as dazzling in their clarity. The entities with which he peopled the transcendent world were none other than these thrones and principalities, powers and dominions enumerated by the Apostle Paul. This identification of impersonal forces and abstractions with more concrete and positive figures had the effect of attenuating the abstract character of the entities of Origen's imagination. They now hovered, vague and indeterminate, between abstraction and being. It would be idle to give them more definite meaning.

What are the characteristics of these transcendent beings? They are pure and innocent, as we see from *De Principiis* I, chap. 8, and more particularly from fragment 15 of the Greek text reproduced in the Koetschau edition. They are endowed with reason. Origen calls them intelligences, rational essences. They possess free-will, as he attempts to prove in *De Principiis*, I, 5, 3. The heavenly bodies also—which, like all his contemporaries, he regards as living— are possessed of freedom (*Ibidem* I, 7, 3 and 4). Finally, they are incorporeal. This latter characteristic was not in accord with the ideas of Rufinus and his contemporaries of Rome. According to him, the Trinity alone is altogether without body. Spirits possess a body, however tenuous and ethereal. Consequently, Rufinus was unable to accept Origen's affirmation; on this point he attempted to rectify the text he translated. A critical comparison of his version with such fragments of the original Greek as are in our possession, leaves no doubt whatsoever as to the deliberate perversion of the text of Origen by his translator. See *De Principiis* I, the whole of chapter 7, in Koetschau's edition.

In this transcendent world there takes place a rebellion which brings about the fall of the rebels ; this fall, as we shall see, is the initial cause of the appearance of the visible world.

It is worthy of note that this idea of a fall, with the suprasensible world as its theatre, is utterly alien to purely Greek systems. We find no mention of it in either Plato, Plutarch or Plotinus. All the same, it appears in every system of Christian origin ; it forms even the one preëminent and outstanding event. Remember the speculations of Valentinus, of the Coptic Gnostics and many others. Consequently it was Christianity that gave birth to the idea of a fall, and it was under the influence of the story of Genesis that it was conceived.

What was the cause of the fall? On this point, Valentinus was very definite. According to him, its first cause was the overweaning desire of Sophia, the thirtieth Aeon, to know God. Her curiosity impelled her to overstep the bounds assigned to her weakness. Origen is less precise. Certainly he declares that, under the instigation of one of the angelic beings, the " intelligences " or entities endowed with reason rebelled and refused to obey God, though he does not say what was their motive in doing so. In a certain passage, he contents himself with the vague declaration that they grew tired of beholding God. One thing certain is that these beings, still wholly spiritual, enjoyed full liberty.

Contrary to all expectation, this fall had as its consequence the appearance of the Cosmos, of bodies, and of flesh. This is a thing that Rufinus did not—or would not—understand. In his version, Origen's meaning has been obscured. To discover what he really thought, we must fall back upon the extracts from the letter of Justinian, the anathemas of the Council of A.D. 553, and the extracts from Jerome's letter to Avitus. The idea that the catastrophe which took place in the transcendent world was the cause of the appearance of the visible Cosmos, was very clearly taught by Valentinus. He insisted on this more than did Origen, declaring that the four passions of Sophia sprang from the four elements. The latter had only to enter into various combinations in order to form the Cosmos.

Along with the Cosmos there appear what Origen calls "the corporeal natures". These are men and animals, beings possessed of a body. Nevertheless, says our theologian, bodies are not all the same. They are, if the expression may be used, more or less body. Corporeity differs in beings. In one, it is opaque and dark; in another, it is more ethereal and luminous.

COSMOLOGY

The reason for this diversity is a moral one. The corporeity of a being varies according to the degree of its culpability. All suprasensible beings that have fallen are clothed in bodies. But in the case of the heavenly beings, whose fault was but slight, the matter of their bodies is tenuous, diaphanous, luminous. The archangels have a little more of matter. Mankind has the body with which we are all acquainted. The daimons have a dense and tenebrous body.

The beings or spirits of the transcendent world, however, did not become corporeal all at once. There is an intermediate stage between spirit and body, one which receives the name of "soul" or ψυχή.[1] The psyche participates of both natures. Note that Origen borrows this term, psyche, from Aristotle. We find it in the theology of Valentinus and of other Gnostics. Men are classified as spiritual, psychic and hylic. The psychic are intermediary, and so are susceptible of ascending or descending, of rising to the rank of the spiritual or falling to that of the material. These psychics are possessed of freewill. The fallen beings, however, speedily fall lower still; one might say that the weight of their wrong-doing drags them down. They assume bodies. Certain are even hurled into

[1] Concerning this notion of the soul, see *De Princ.*, I, 8, 1 Koetschau's edition.

the abyss and become daimons. The ultimate term of this tragic fall constitutes matter. Logically, matter should be regarded as evil. Origen, on one occasion at least, went to the extent of calling it impure (*In Joh.*, XX, 16).

We can now examine as a whole the immense chain of beings which stretches from the transcendent world to the ultimate confines of the visible world. On the summit, all around God, are the entities endowed with reason, beings of the invisible world. These are pure spirits, or intelligences, as Origen prefers to call them in the Greek fragments. The entities, tired of being perfect, and led astray by one of their own number, who will be called the Devil, rebelled. Thereupon begins the fall, a revolution which is to give a new aspect to all things. The condition—consequent on its rebellion—of each entity varies according to the degree of culpability. Some become simply " souls ", their fall does not carry them lower. This is not definitely stated by Origen, though his logic and language both imply it. It is unnecessary to penetrate into his thought too closely, for this is a domain over which imagination has greater sway than reason has. Other entities assume a more or less dense or luminous body. Those that become men are capable of falling lower still. Remembering what Plato says, Origen declares that they become animals, even beings devoid of intelligence. The last stage of abasement is the condition of the daimon.

Thus, throughout this conception, a wholly moral cause determines the existence and condition of beings. Had evil not appeared, the Cosmos and its inhabitants would never have come into existence. In the *Timaeus*, it is metaphysics that supplies the philosopher with the rationale of the Cosmos and with the explanation of its appearance; it is both metaphysics and morals that supply Origen with the principle of existence of his Cosmos.

Once this is firmly established, Origen evidently thinks he has dealt with the essentials of cosmology; the rest is of no great importance in his eyes. The rest is simply the rational explanation of the formation, continuance and evolution of the Cosmos, questions that are of little interest, as we have seen, to the thinkers of the time, whether philosophers, Gnostic theologians or Christian doctors. To discover what Origen thinks of them and thus to acquire a fairly complete cosmology, it would be necessary to quote a few texts scattered at random throughout his works.

The Stoics have taught him the idea of the organic unity of the Cosmos. Like them, he calls it a " living being ".

It is one because it is a living being; it is diverse because the beings that people it are themselves as diverse as the faults that have brought about their ruin.

When Origen reflects on the persistence and duration of the Cosmos, he is content to repeat with the Stoics that there is a divine principle immanent in the Cosmos. This is the Logos, a principle which, as Stoicism taught, prevails throughout the Cosmos and in mankind. This suffices for our theologian, who does not enquire how this Cosmos is organised, what laws it obeys. He never dreams of questioning the Cosmos itself to make it give up its secret. In the whole of his chapter on cosmology, there is not a single observation of fact.

This Cosmos, he says, had a beginning. His explanation of the origin of the Universe as well as the Bible account of Creation, even allegorically interpreted, demand this, and our theologian did not fail to demonstrate it formally. Consequently it will have an end. What will this end be? Before disappearing, our Cosmos will undergo more than one transformation. The present Cosmos will be succeeded by another which will be followed by a third. There will be a plurality of worlds. Origen did not invent this conception; it had previously been formulated by Plutarch in his *De oraculorum*

COSMOLOGY 91

defectu. And before him, the Stoics taught that the Cosmos is periodically consumed by fire, to reappear subsequently in the same form. Origen has quite different reasons for adopting the idea of the plurality of worlds, reasons of a moral order; and it is this characteristic that explains the differences we discover between his doctrine and that of the philosophers. We shall return to this aspect subsequently.

Nevertheless, this succession of worlds will not be indefinite. Origen declares that there will be a " consummation " of things. What is his conception of this? Will the material Cosmos be gradually absorbed back again into spirit? Will matter finally be eliminated? Will the end consist in a re-establishment of the beginning? Will the Cosmos and its drama have been, as it were, only an episode which would not have come about if the beings of the invisible world had not fallen?

This would appear to be stated in more than one text of Origen. And yet on this point he is obscure and hesitant. Manifestly he is strongly inclined to believe in the disappearance of the visible Cosmos, for he announces (*In Joh.*, XIX, 22) with joy and gladness the coming of a spiritual Cosmos (κόσμος νοητός), the beauty of which will delight and ravish the pure. Then " God will be all in all ". This point, however, will be discussed when dealing with our theologian's doctrine of final things.

Considered as a whole this cosmology of Origen would seem to be of very composite source, composed as it is of elements borrowed from Plato and Aristotle, from Stoicism and from the great Gnostic theologians. Of all the influences that made up his doctrine of the Universe, it is the Biblical influence that is least pronounced. The only trait which Origen retained is the idea of a fall which took place at the beginning. No wonder it appeared the most heretical of his doctrines and that his detractors made it the chief head of their accusations.

It must be added that, in Origen's writings, this doctrine does not appear as clear and logical as in the exposition here given. Our theologian was not free—as was a Basilides or a Valentinus—to build up his conception of the Universe by entirely eliminating the Christian tradition, or taking it into account only to the extent he pleased. He is obliged to uphold certain Biblical and Christian ideas which did not agree with his own conception, bringing into it irregularities, even contradictions. Quite naturally, Origen endeavours to mitigate them, even to dispense with them altogether. The allegorical method offered him means of doing this—which means were almost always efficacious.

COSMOLOGY

All the same, certain data remained irreducible; e.g. the current belief that God is the maker of heaven and earth. In his commentaries, Origen attempts to prove that this Biblical affirmation has a limited signification.

It simply denotes that God is the creator of the suprasensible world and the rational spirits, i.e. the beings of the invisible world. The Scriptures never meant that God moulded with His hands this matter, the mere contact with which would defile Him. But when Origen is defending the Bible tradition against Celsus, he finds himself compelled to abandon this restriction, and upholds the belief current among the Christians (*C. Celsum*, IV, 54). Could Origen deny that God is the creator of matter? To admit this is infinitely repugnant to him. Ultimately he goes so far as to admit that God created—not matter as it exists and as we know it, but—the essence of matter, matter still in the rough, devoid of those qualities it is subsequently to assume, the ὕλη ἄποιος, as the philosophers called it. And what is to be said of the current assertion that the Logos was the creative instrument of God? Is this the function that Origen habitually assigns to it? Were not matter and bodies to appear along with evil? In order not to exclude the Logos from the work of creation, Origen, recalling Plato, teaches that the Logos created the world according to the archetypes which are in God.

On huge glaciers are sometimes to be seen erratic masses which stain their otherwise immaculate whiteness. How did they come to be on that vast stretch of snow and ice? The beliefs which Origen could not put aside because they were imbedded in tradition resemble these erratic masses; they stand out distinct from his thought, spoiling and distorting its harmonious and logical order and sequence.

Whatever the concessions he made to Christian beliefs in the matter of cosmology, it is manifest that his cosmology was closely related to that of the philosophers of his time; it could not repudiate its Platonico-Stoic origin. Even without incurring the charge of malevolence, one might affirm that there was no longer anything Christian about it. So thought Origen's detractors, and it was for this reason that they directed the shafts of their criticism upon his cosmological teachings. And yet, can it be imagined that the Platonists, Pythagoreans or Stoics of that time would have recognised in this doctrine a conception born of their own thought? This is very doubtful. More probably the doctrine would have disconcerted them. Beneath its philosophical garb, they would have discerned a substance foreign to them. Their

COSMOLOGY

cosmology was essentially—even exclusively—metaphysical; that of Origen was not only metaphysical, it was also moral.

It was not so much by logical as by ethical reasons that Origen explained its successive phases. When closely examined, indeed, his cosmology was a moral and religious interpretation of the Cosmos such as might have been conceived by a philosopher who had studied both Platonism and Stoicism. Whence could he have had the idea of such an explanation of the Universe, if not from Christianity? In spite of appearances, the cosmological doctrine of Origen was fundamentally of Christian inspiration

It would have been too much to expect Jerome and Rufinus, Justinian and the Fathers of the Council of A.D. 553, to make the distinction here mentioned. At the utmost, they would have understood that this doctrine, whatever it might be, did not affect the essence of Christianity, which, if necessary, could dispense with any explanation of the origin of the Cosmos. Is any trace of it to be found in the teaching of Jesus? The Apostle Paul alludes to a cosmological doctrine which indeed appears to originate in Rabbinical theology, but did this doctrine form part of the structure of his faith? After all, its place is on the periphery of Christianity, the vital parts of which it does not concern.

On this particular point, indeed, Origen was able to reconcile his Christian faith with philosophy. Instead of injuring each other, they afford mutual support, and enable the intellectuals of the age to understand that it is possible to be both a philosopher and a Christian at the same time.

CHRISTOLOGY

CHRISTOLOGY

BEFORE stating the Christological doctrine of Origen, it would be worth while to mention those of his writings which more particularly deal with this question.

First, there are the first two volumes of the commentary on John, those that exist of the commentary on Matthew, the first two books in the *Contra Celsum*, and finally the treatise on prayer. These are the original sources; we possess none other except in Latin versions.

There are various chapters of the first two books of the *De Principiis*, the two books of the commentary on *Solomon's Song*, translated by Rufinus, and the two homilies on the same book in the remarkable version of Jerome. It is scarcely necessary to state that these Latin versions should be used only after they have been subjected to severe criticism. As we see, the sources of Origen's Christological doctrine are plentiful, and there is no serious difficulty in obtaining from them his authentic doctrine.

The doctrine of the Logos, at that time current

among most philosophers, constitutes the very essence of our author's Christology.[1]

In the early centuries of the Christian era, there came about a curious fusion of Platonism and Stoicism. The two philosophies gave each other mutual aid. In Platonism, the transcendence of God was such that it became more and more difficult to suppose that He exercised any action whatsoever upon the Cosmos or upon mankind.

The gulf which separated this God—Who was increasingly relegated to the abstract—from the visible world, continually widened. The need of one or more intermediaries became more and more apparent. In the *Timaeus*, the master himself had actually assigned a rôle as interpreter to the soul of the world. Stoicism could know nothing of this difficulty or consequently of the need of an intermediary between God and the Cosmos, seeing that it regarded God as immanent in the Cosmos. He found Himself an interior influence, in direct contact with the visible world. To this divine principle Stoicism gave the name of Logos. When considered in its several manifestations, it used the term in the plural. Was not the idea of

---

[1] On the history of the doctrine of the Logos, the excellent book of Heinze is still the classic work. It need only be supplemented by that of Aal on the same subject.

CHRISTOLOGY

regarding this Logos as the intermediary between the absolute God and the Cosmos bound to present itself to men's minds sooner or later? It was this very thing that happened. Platonism had long ago appropriated the Logos of the Stoics, to make thereof the intermediary it needed. This Logos was altogether divine without being identified with the supreme God, and on the other hand it was interior to the Cosmos, consequently in direct contact with it: a very elegant way of blending Platonism with Stoicism. The God of Plato remained the absolute and inaccessible God, and though the God of the Stoics occupied a subordinate rank, He had the advantage of still being the very spring and energy of the Cosmos. Thus detached from the one supreme God, while sharing His nature, the Logos could assume the most varied aspects. Its sphere of influence necessarily assumed the most diverse forms. At one time it was envisaged in the variety of its action, and called logoi or forces. At another it was designated by terms which emphasised its abstract nature or its philosophical character; and yet again it was represented in more concrete form. Philo of Alexandria gives the name of angels to the principles and the divine forces scattered throughout the Cosmos; Plutarch calls them daimons.

This diversity of characters in the Logos is not the main essence of the notion. The essential element is its rôle or function as intermediary. Consequently the Logos is always subordinate, in the second rank. It can be only a δεύτερος θεός. This is the distinctive feature of the philosophical doctrine of the Logos, the sign by which the doctrine is recognised. As a result, the Christian theologians who adopted it and who identified this Logos—which they borrowed from philosophy—with the "Lord", always regard this latter as subordinate to God. He is God, though a god on the second plane. They are of necessity subordinationists. This is how things stand with the Gnostic theologians, with Clement of Alexandria and with Origen. Though the Christian theologian may have lost the definite philosophical meaning of the term Logos, if he applies it to Jesus, he experiences not the slightest difficulty in regarding the Son as on an equality with the Father. Indeed, this term is no longer for him anything but a verbal formula; it has lost its true signification. What matter though it be expanded to the point of destroying the boundaries between the absolute God and the god of the second rank; nothing will any longer prevent this theologian from being a consubstantialist. This is how it was with all the trinitarian theologians of the

CHRISTOLOGY

fourth century. Origen is still too much imbued with philosophy to forget the meaning it attributed to the term Logos. Indeed, it is absurd to bring as a grievance against him the charge of having been a subordinationist. In his time, one could not help being one.

Origen regards this Logos as the essential element of his Christological doctrine. Previous to his time, the Logos had been identified with the Lord, both by the author of the fourth Gospel and by the writer of the so-called Pauline Epistles of the Captivity. But this Logos, adopted by the early Christians, is not exactly the Logos of the philosophers; it is a convenient term which enables them to enhance the divinity of Jesus Christ. It must not be regarded as anything more. This Logos has a meaning which is rather mystical and religious than cosmological or metaphysical. The Logos as Origen understands it is the true Logos of philosophical tradition, of which it possesses all the characteristics. It existed long before Jesus Christ, and was at first quite independent of him. It has always been God, the divine principle immanent in the Cosmos. Further, the Logos has been the instrumental cause of the existence of the Cosmos, and continues to be the divine force which maintains its life and constitutes its organic unity. From it emanates the life of beings, whether spirits, souls or men. It draws this life from the bosom of God and transmits it to the beings in descending scales. Consequently, it does really play the part of the "second god". The philosophical source of this Logos of Origen is manifest, as may be seen from the following references: *In Joh.*, XX, 16, *C. Celsum*, IV, 15, *In Joh.*, II, 1; II, 2; II, 17; XIII, 36.

One day, this Logos becomes a man. What is it exactly that this means? What does Origen understand by incarnation? Our theologian is continually declaring that the Son of God who is none other than the Logos has "taken or assumed" a being that has a human soul and body. It has blended with and appropriated to itself a real man, and has thus become Christ Jesus. Jesus is the man who has incorporated the Son of God. Man consists of soul and body, and it must not be forgotten that Origen uses the term "soul" in the Aristotelian sense.

This is not the soul as understood in the *Phaedo*, where it is intermediary between the body and the spirit. A man just as he is, in a simple, crude state, if we may thus express ourselves, a man previous to all determination, who is neither good nor bad: such was the being chosen by the Logos. Such is Jesus, the son of Mary.

CHRISTOLOGY

This is no simple human body adopted by the Son of God for his earthly habitation. He, the second god, makes choice and adoption of a complete man with whom to blend and mingle. In the Greek texts, Origen strongly insists on this particular meaning of what is called the Incarnation.

Once this point is understood, all the other Christological affirmations of Origen become perfectly clear. Thus, the Logos or Son of God who has united to himself Jesus, the son of Mary, loses nothing of his own nature through this union; he simply cohabits with Jesus and remains himself. So independent is he that, according to Origen, it is permissible for him to leave the man he has chosen, to absent himself, to return and again take up his associate. See the commentary on John (XIX, 6). Since he is immortal and divine, he cannot die. It is not he who hangs upon the cross; he has departed. It is Jesus who endures the death agony. See *Contra Celsum*, VII, 16. It is not the Logos or Son of God who suffers and moans in the Garden of Olives; it is the man Jesus.

And yet, however independent of the man Jesus the Son of God may be, he forms one single being with him. Origen distinctly affirms the organic unity of Christ Jesus. This is not the Logos and Jesus in juxtaposition; it is one personality. See *Contra Celsum*, II, 9. The result of this is that the man Jesus becomes transformed by contact with the Logos. Origen goes so far as to say that his mortal body and his human soul become transmuted into divinity.

It would assuredly be an easy matter to pick out the incoherencies and contradictions inseparable from such a conception. What advantage would be gained? Is it not more profitable and more interesting to try to understand Origen, to find an adequate explanation of this conception of his. It must be remembered that he is a Greek, imbued with the Greek spirit. Now, for a Greek of this age, the idea of a god who assumes human nature, who becomes a real man, and after a time abandons the man with whom he has identified himself, is quite a usual one. Naturally, so long as he forms one with this man, he bestows on him some reflection of his beauty, even of his divinity. It does not seem a matter of surprise to this Greek that a god should indulge the fancy of disguising himself as a man and appearing among human beings. Any one might meet him and discover from certain signs that he is face to face with deity. There are human beings who are gods in disguise. The perfect Christian, said Clement of Alexandria, becomes a god (IV *Strom.*, XXIII, 149).

This conception, familiar enough to the

CHRISTOLOGY

Hellenic mind, is quite foreign to the Occidental. A Latin regards the gods as always retaining something of their primitive character; they have remained abstractions. The idea of deity in flesh and blood, talking to and moving amongst men, was neither familiar nor natural to a spiritual son of Rome. Consequently, in the West it was said that the Son of God had simply assumed a body, put on mortal flesh.

This act was called by the Greeks the humanisation of the Son of God, ἐνανθρώπησις, and by the Latins " incarnation ", incorporation. To attribute to Origen the idea that the Logos or Son of God has put on flesh or a body which is not a man, would be to pervert his meaning. Say that he believes the body or flesh of man, which the Son of God appropriates, to be of superior quality and therefore worthy of him, and you will be repeating what he maintains in his controversy with Celsus. But do not forget that, along with this body or flesh, the Logos also assumes a soul, a ψυχή.

What afterwards, according to Origen, is the function of the Logos Jesus? As we have seen, before his humanisation or incarnation, the Logos or Son of God had a supreme rôle. He was the creative instrument of the Cosmos, he was its organic principle, and he constituted the vital energy of mankind.

Origen, following Clement of Alexandria, supplemented this wholly philosophical conception of the function of the Logos, by adding that this Logos or Son of God had inspired the prophets and was immanent in them; his influence amongst men themselves had been spiritual as well as cosmic. But what was his rôle when he became the Logos Jesus? This Origen expounds at length in his commentary on John (I, 16 to 39). He considers that this rôle was an extremely diversified one.

His function assumed many aspects; this it was that enabled him really to be the Saviour of men. He was able to adapt himself to diverse souls, to make himself all things to all men. Origen finds the proof of what he advocates in the fact that the terms used by sacred writers to designate the Son of God are many and varied. In the Old Testament there are the divers Messianic appellations; in the New Testament, the Johannine writings abound in names that denote the Son of God: the lamb, the vine, the bread, the truth, the life, the resurrection, the Logos, the door, the way.

And in other places was he not called the wisdom, the propitiation, "the first and the last"? Origen examines all these terms; each is used in order to throw light on some aspect of the influence of the Son of God since he

CHRISTOLOGY

became the Logos Jesus. In a general way, this influence incites to good, trains and evolves souls, and redeems. *Qua* good shepherd, Christ Jesus leads men; *qua* light, he illumines them; *qua* vine, he inebriates them with the wine of the Ideal; he enables them to contemplate eternal Ideas, models and types; he is the master of ecstasy. This work of the Logos Jesus is adapted to the different categories of mankind. He transmits divine life to " gods ", to " thrones ", to " angels ", as he does to men. To simple believers, he is the Saviour *qua* the crucified one; to the more advanced, he is the light-giver who brings them into direct contact with the Father. In a word, the Christ or Logos Jesus is the great intermediary, the dispenser of all light and life, the evolver of mind and spirit, the mystagogue who introduces men to the transcendent world, the initiator into the supreme Gnosis. Origen found all these characters of the Christ expressed and illustrated in *Solomon's Song*. His famous allegorical commentary on this sacred writing was a kind of hymn composed in honour of his Christ—a hymn whose mystical lyricism filled Saint Jerome with admiration.

According to this conception, what finally becomes of the humanity of Jesus Christ?

On the one hand, Origen asserts his divinity with the utmost clearness. The Logos or Son of God is very real in his eyes; by definition he is god. Unquestionably, he is not interchangeable with the Father, but though subordinate to Him, he is divine. On the other hand, the man assumed by the Logos is no less real; as Origen expressly declares on many occasions. Consequently, he rejects both the idea that Jesus Christ is just a man and the Docetic doctrine which reduced his humanity to mere appearance.

What, after all, does he retain of the Gospel story? From what point of view does he regard it?

Here we are not without documentary instruction. In his *True Word*, Celsus makes a thorough criticism of the Gospel narrative. Origen replies in detail and at considerable length. The theory upheld by Celsus is by no means the one we should have supposed or expected.

It is not as a rationalist that he criticises the Gospel narrative. The fault he finds with the whole story is that it is not marvellous enough. What it relates concerning Jesus is not worthy of a god. The miracles attributed to him are not sufficiently dazzling and wonderful. He is even represented in piteous guise. Look at him in the Garden of Olives, moaning and weeping; is that the attitude of a god? In a word, there is nothing divine about this Jesus; he is an

CHRISTOLOGY

average sort of person devoid of prestige or *éclat*. The Christians have been very ill inspired to choose him as the patron of their religion. There were other individuals they might have preferred before him. In order to prove his theory, Celsus attempts to depreciate as much as possible the Gospel facts; instead of finding fault with them for being miraculous, he considers that there is not enough of the miracle about them, seeing that they are the actions of a god. Origen's defence consists in maintaining the very reverse of the argument of Celsus; he enhances still further all the wonder involved in the story of the Magi.

These wise men from the East understood that an extraordinary event was about to take place, because they had perceived that the daimons were greatly perturbed. The star of Bethlehem becomes the occasion for exalting the supernatural character of the story—a character which he retains. Sometimes Origen is considerably embarrassed. Is not the Passion a disturbing element? What can he reply to Celsus, who regards it as proof of the insignificance of Jesus? Very fortunately Origen is resourceful enough to declare that it is the man Jesus—not the Son of God—who moans and suffers. Naturally, the stories of the resurrection enable him to take his revenge. Do they not admirably illustrate the divine nature of Jesus Christ? The result is that our theologian retains all the material facts of the Gospel story which enhance the prestige of Jesus, such as the tales of his childhood, the miracles, the resurrections, the transfiguration, the resurrection of Jesus Christ himself.

The eight volumes of the commentary on Matthew that have come down to us give an account of what he thought regarding the sermons, the parables and sayings of Jesus. Almost invariably he gives them an allegorical interpretation. He is more eager and anxious to regard them as illustrations of his doctrines than to discover their real and particular meaning. As a result, he does not grasp their true originality. In this sense, it is correct to say that he did not understand the Jesus Christ who really lived, acted and spoke. He offers us the paradoxical example of a man who is imbued with the purest Christian spirit and yet does not know what Jesus of Nazareth was and what he really intended to do. To sum up, he retains the material character of the Gospel facts, which he is free to interpret as he pleases. Once he had made up his mind to remain faithful to the living tradition of the Churches, he could not carry freedom of interpretation any farther. Allegorist though he was, he never dreamt

CHRISTOLOGY

of giving up the historicity of the Gospel narrative.

Considered in itself, in its essential nature, the whole of this Christology of Origen is nothing else than a learned justification of the Christian belief of his time. There can be no doubt of the affinity between the common faith in Christ held by the Christians of the third century, and the doctrine of Origen. The reason why, at the end of the fourth century, it was possible to accuse him of heresy, was because in the interval the common faith in Christ had become modified; it had taken on a dogmatic precision which debased it considerably. Men believed they had remained faithful to tradition, whereas they had deviated considerably from it. Consequently we think it right to say that the doctrine we have expounded is an interpretation in philosophical terms of the faith in the "Lord" which was current at the time. Origen, in full sincerity, was able to commune with confessors and martyrs. Did not he himself suffer like them and for the same faith?

We may wonder whether his discussions on the nature of the Christ, the elements which constitute this nature, his relations on the one hand with the Father and on the other with beings of lower rank, would impassion the modern Christian, to whatsoever confession he might belong. Doubtless these discussions are far from being as subtil and abstruse as they came to be in the fourth and fifth centuries. But would they not still be too subtle and abstruse for the convinced militant Christian of these days?

What is the first thing this Christian requires of Christ and his Gospel? Is it an explanation of the creation of the Universe? Definite teaching on the origin of evil? A dogmatic explanation of the relations between God and Christ, the Father and the Son? Is it even a learned formula of the doctrine of Redemption or of the authority of the Scriptures? Are not his thoughts and pre-occupations more positive, his engrossing interests more practical?

What does the most earnest and ardent Christian of the day seek in the Gospel, or expect of Christ, if not, above all else, a rule of life and the practical means of applying this rule? He reminds us in striking fashion of the best of the contemporaries of Clement of Alexandria and of Origen.

These went in crowds to the philosophers to learn how a sage, a man, ought to live. They did not ask for the secret of the Cosmos, but rather for a rule of conduct ($\beta\prime os$). Justin Martyr relates that he made a tour of the schools of the various philosophers. A Pythagorean

CHRISTOLOGY

declares to him that, previous to teaching him his philosophy, he would himself have to receive instruction in mathematics and astronomy. Justin turns away, for he is eager to know how he ought to act in life itself, when he is confronted with tribulation, with sickness and death.

The Christian of the present day, who is one both by conviction and by vocation, first demands for himself, as an individual, a principle of guidance which is imperative for his conscience, his feelings, his will, and which thus fashions and moulds his very life.

A very distinct end to pursue here below is what he ardently desires and requires, above all else, of the religion he professes. And he has the same requirements for collective life, society, the nation, humanity as a whole. For society he demands moral direction, just as for the individual. He considers that collective bodies also should have superior ends to aim at, and that human evolution should pursue a certain goal, which is called the Ideal, or the Kingdom of God. Lastly he relies upon religious faith to procure for mankind the energies exacted by the application of his ideal of life.

Most assuredly, in the eyes of the modern Christian, other things are not without importance. He understands the utility—even the necessity—of possessing clear and well-reasoned doctrines. To his mind, however, the application of his Christian ideal is more important than more theoretical matters.

To this Christian, evidently, Origen's point of view will appear too intellectualistic, too doctrinaire. How could it be otherwise, since what he asks of Christianity is not a superior religious philosophy, but rather a line of conduct, of action and life, along with the secret of its real and practical application?

Still, we must beware of overlooking the expediency of Origen's effort, nay, of its necessity at the time it was made. Up to that day, all Christians looked upon the Gospel not as a theory, a doctrine, ideas, but as beliefs, precepts, an ideal of life. Admirable in action, firm in belief and heroic in faith, they were very feeble from the standpoint of ideas, of doctrine, of thought. In the long run, this inadequacy would certainly have become injurious. For the defence as well as for the propagation of the Christian faith, a strong intellectual equipment was indispensable. One had to be able to confront the philosophers with what these latter called dogmas (δόγματα.) Along with Clement his master, Origen saw this, and with incomparable valour set to work. This is why he made it his purpose to supplement faith in Christ with a Christological doctrine.

CHRISTOLOGY

What is equally admirable is that this necessity of formulating a learned Christology did not prevent him from insisting very powerfully on the moral and spiritual influence of his Logos Jesus. No one of his time had a broader conception of this influence; on its reality he bases his principal apologetic argument. Whereas Celsus systematically vilified the Jesus of the Gospels, calling him an ordinary person and quite unworthy of the rôle imposed upon him by the Christians, Origen set forth the fruitful influence, so productive of moral life and heroism, which this Jesus Christ was exercising, more than two centuries after his coming. Was he not daily weening men from Paganism, transforming them, making them, if necessary, confessors and martyrs? Celsus wanted certain and sure proofs of the moral greatness of Jesus. They existed. He had only to open his eyes; he would find them amongst the Christians.

The Christian thinker who was able to discern so correctly the genuine secret of the power of his Christ, was no simple theorist, however abstruse might be his Christological doctrine. In him, the significance of life formed one with the virtuosity of the logician. Herein lay his originality.

THE DOCTRINE OF REDEMPTION

THE DOCTRINE OF REDEMPTION

THE end of the first century of the Christian era heralds the coming of a genuine religious revival. It continues to grow and expand. Striking is the contrast between this period and the preceding one from this point of view. At the time of Cicero, Scepticism is prevalent everywhere. At Rome, if one is not a Pyrrhonist, one is at least an Epicurean or a disciple of Carneades and the New Academy. A century later, Scepticism is utterly discredited. A sure sign of this is the increasing unpopularity of Epicurus and his school, even among the philosophers. In his letters to Lucilius, Seneca takes malicious pleasure in citing and praising certain maxims of Epicurus. Who would have thought that this denier, this atheist, this friend of pleasure, had left behind him sentences and maxims worthy to be remembered? In the days of Lucian, the word Epicurean was synonymous with atheist. To overwhelm the Christians with obloquy, their names were linked with the Epicureans. The admiration which Lucian of Samosata bestowed on Epicurus is quite exceptional.

In Rome, under the instigation of the Emperor Augustus, the national legends are extolled and the official cult restored to honour. Virgil and Livy are the Emperor's mouth-pieces, the interpreters of the new order. The time will soon be ripe for the worship of Roma, for that of the Divi, and before long in the provinces the cult of the living Prince will be the most popular of all. At the same time, the syncretistic religions of the East, of Syria, Phrygia, Egypt, Babylon and Persia, become known throughout the Empire. The mysteries enjoy a great revival of popularity. Who would have the courage to refrain from becoming initiated? Did not Lucian state that this was the grievance urged against the philosopher Demonax in Athens? He had to explain his position before the assembly. Finally, never had astrology and demonology, oracles and predictions, been more in the ascendant. Everybody believed in them. Such a critic as Celsus has not the courage to repudiate them. Lucian of Samosata was almost the only man who had the boldness to do so. Like Plutarch, Origen believes in daimons and in the influence of the constellations. There were innumerable signs pointing to the fact that the minds of men were turning more and more in the direction of religion.

This fervid religious sentiment of the second

and third centuries has attracted considerable attention among critics and historians. On the whole, it may be that it is regarded too seriously. It was certainly a cloak for a great deal of superstition. Charlatanism excelled in exploiting the credulity and the terrors of the devout. Interested hypocrisy had free scope and indulged its fancy; imposters were rampant. Lucian and Celsus more particularly reveal to us these lower aspects of the religious revival of the period. Alexander of Abonoteichos and Peregrinus, whose portraits, as sketched by Lucian, are no doubt somewhat highly coloured, must be in truth very real characters. And yet there existed choice souls whose religious aspirations were most earnest and sincere. They felt the need of purification and expiation, of redemption and immortality, to a degree unknown in the classic age. These mystical needs called for satisfaction by liturgical rites and gestures, by sacred formulas, by initiations and sacrifices. It was really at this period that we first hear of the idea of the efficacy of sacrament, of the *opus operatum*.

It has been remarked that now, for the first time in the Hellenic world, religion becomes individualistic. Concern is felt regarding individual salvation. In the classic religions, the individual was utterly forgotten; in the syncretistic religions, he is in the forefront, the most important element.

Upon this wholly new tendency another speedily grafted itself, of a more particular and less general nature. The drama of salvation grew and expanded until it embraced the Universe. In certain apostolic writings we witness the birth of the idea of cosmic redemption. Paul had already expressed this idea in the eighth chapter of his Epistle to the Romans, and it is clearly formulated and expanded in his Epistles to the Colossians and to the Ephesians. It becomes general amongst the Gnostics; their theologians cannot imagine a redemption which does not embrace the Cosmos, Basilides, Valentinus and his disciples, the Gnostics of the *Philosophumena*, the authors of the *Pistis Sophia* and of the Coptic *Jeu*, all indulge in dreams of universal redemption. It is from this point of view that they explain the evolution of the Cosmos and its destiny.

It is this same tendency that Origen follows; his conception of redemption is not simply individual, it is cosmic. Logically, it should culminate in universal salvation.

His doctrine of redemption is conditioned by that of the fall. We remember that this takes place first in the transcendent world, among the suprasensible entities, or, as he expresses himself in the fragments of the *De Principiis*, "the incorporeal intelligences", νόες. The falls are more or less profound. Degrees of culpability vary, causing diversity of fall. The result is a succession of ever more serious falls, a tragic progression into evil. This constitutes a gradual sinking into matter, which at each stage becomes ever more dense. It is a chain of the damned, stretching from the still luminous and diaphanous constellations on to the dark and opaque daimons. These are at the bottom of the abyss.

The relationship between this conception of the fall and that of the Gnostic masters is apparent. All the same, there is one important difference. Origen declares emphatically that both the fall and the falls are the result of free-will. Suprasensible beings have willed that this should be; there has been no compulsion. The Gnostic theologians look upon the fall, which subsequently has its repercussions from stage to stage right on to the end, as inevitable. In their system there is no question of freedom. The fall had to come about, otherwise the Cosmos would not have existed. From the moment that matter and the Cosmos were to appear, this transcendent evolution could not be avoided. It is doubtful whether the Gnostic theologians recognised that their conception excluded moral freedom; they do not appear to have asked themselves the question. Origen, however, clearly saw that they were sacrificing their freedom, and he determined to safeguard it.

Quite naturally, Origen's doctrine of redemption and that of the Gnostic theologians present analogous differences and resemblances. In the system of Valentinus, as in that of the Naassenes, the Perates and the Sethites of the *Philosophumena*, redemption consists in the return of the divine elements which have gone astray into impure matter. A movement takes place in the opposite direction; the luminous particles are once more re-absorbed into God. This is how Origen conceives of redemption. One might say that, at a given moment, the fall of beings comes to a halt; they seem to have reached the bottom of the abyss. Then they ascend and, stage by stage, return to their primitive state. The daimons—theoretically at least—again become men; these rise to the state of ψυχαί (souls), and at last, from being souls they are transformed anew into pure intelligences (νόες) or entities endowed with reason. Finally, matter disappears; the original order is restored: " God is all in all ".

At first sight, Origen's system of redemption is of like nature with that of most of the Gnostic masters. Nevertheless, it differs considerably from them. According to Origen, moral free-

DOCTRINE OF REDEMPTION

dom plays in redemption the same rôle as in the fall. The beings that ascend are consenting beings; there is nothing inevitable about their return to God. Whereas, in the Gnostic systems, the return to the principle of all things follows a sort of rhythm whose regularity is undisturbed and all its phases foreseen, in the mind of Origen, redemption is speedy or tardy according to the progress of each one. Here is a man who ascends to God at a single bound, so to speak. His sojourn on this earth will suffice for his complete development. And here is another who will detach himself from his terrestrial nature but slowly; he will have need of more than one life on earth. In the *Pistis Sophia*, the path which is to bring back the entity that has gone astray, to its place in the pleroma, is marked out in advance; the hindrances are anticipated; the means of overcoming obstacles are well known. It will be necessary to make a certain gesture, utter some formula or prayer, for the doors to be opened one after another. Quite otherwise does our theologian, following the fourth Gospel, depict the salvation of the Samaritan woman. She represents the soul that has strayed and is lost. To bring her back to God, Jesus must become her instructor, by persuasion providing illumination at each stage.

The proof that free-will is the corner-stone

of his doctrines both of redemption and of the fall, and that it is the most important element of the entire system, is found in the fact that Origen expressly teaches that beings, once restored to their primitive state, may again relapse, and recommence the same evolution. They at all times possess free self-determination in the direction of evil.

It is also moral freedom that gives its special character to the redemption conceived by our theologian. Since redemption is the effect of freedom, in order that it may come about and that beings may be saved, it is necessary to work upon them by persuasion, to mould and educate them. In the final analysis, education is the method of redemption as understood by Origen. It consists essentially in divine training and guidance. The God of Origen, as we have seen, is an educator; the salvation he wills can be nothing else than an education.

This is a feature which reveals to us that Origen is not only a true Greek, but more especially that his mind was moulded and fashioned by Plato, and perhaps—we should add—by Aristotle. He is profoundly imbued with their system of education. They look upon the formation of a citizen as a matter of training. Origen also looks upon the formation of the perfect Christian as likewise a matter of

DOCTRINE OF REDEMPTION

training. Let him be moulded and fashioned himself by the divine pedagogue, as Clement of Alexandria said, and he will attain to supreme bliss.

In this respect Origen, unknown to himself, is very far from the simple believers of his time. These have the idea that God is above all else a judge, that salvation is the outcome of a sentence or a verdict. Not for a moment do they imagine that redemption could be the work of a divine educator. Equally removed from Gnosticism and from popular Christianity, Origen's doctrine of redemption is quite his own; its originality was even the reason why it was not understood.

We will now consider the inevitable consequences of Origen's point of view.

In the first place, since redemption is conceived as the result of a divine education or training, it is clear that it will require a long period of time. An education cannot be built up in a day; a great deal will depend on the persons to be taught. Some will be more apt and pliable; others more refractory. There will be the greatest diversity. It is conceivable that a small number, whose good will equals their aptitude, may in a single life reach the goal, i.e. the necessary degree of perfection; but these will never be more than a few. What of the masses? Origen knows them well, he cherishes no illusions regarding them. Every page of his homilies tells us what he thinks of simple believers. How ignorant they are! They imagine that God has a body. They are unable to read the Scriptures and know nothing of its allegorical meaning. Like the Jews, they keep to the literal interpretation. Consequently, each of his homilies is a passionate effort to mould and educate these masses. No wonder he had convinced himself that the duration of a single human life was insufficient to complete the redemption of simple believers, as he understood it, at all events. This is why he adopts the doctrine of the plurality of worlds. As already stated, it was not he who invented it; Plutarch also held the belief. But whereas the philosopher of Chaeroneia adopts it because of the requirements of his system, Origen makes it his own because the redemption of the majority of reasonable beings cannot come about apart from a succession of worlds. These latter become schools for human souls. A soul passes from school to school until at last it has come to understand the conditions of its return to God and of its salvation, and has agreed to these conditions.

One other consequence of Origen's point of view is that redemptive education, as he under-

DOCTRINE OF REDEMPTION 131

stands it, will be alike moral and intellectual. He also shows himself faithful to the Hellenic tradition. From its beginnings, philosophy closely linked together morality and intellectual development; it was in accordance with this dual point of view that Socrates took upon himself the task of training the youth. Plato is not content to furnish his sage with certain attainments in knowledge, he insists that he should have a certain character, certain moral qualities. His entire system of education, as expounded in the *Republic* and the *Laws*, tends to the harmonious development of the mind and of the moral nature. Exactly the same end was followed by Aristotle in his *Nicomachean Ethics* and in his *Politics*. The Stoics also, in their turn, adopted and developed the same tradition. Never was it more characteristic of Greek philosophy than during the first few centuries of the Christian era. It becomes a tendency, more and more marked in all the schools, to give up metaphysical speculations, the problem of knowledge, the explanation of the Universe, and to cultivate morality to the exclusion of almost everything else. Consider, for instance, the teachings of Seneca, Musonius, Epictetus, Plutarch, Dion Prusaensis, Maximus Tyrius, Marcus Aurelius, and even of Celsus and Lucian. A philosopher at this period is a man who professes a certain kind of life (βίος). The famous Diogenes is regarded as the philosopher *par excellence*. Epictetus extols him as the perfect model of the sage. The one important question for every reflecting mind is: "What is the best kind of life?" (τίς ὅ ἄριστος βίος). Menippus, according to Lucian, in his work which bears this title, descends even to Hades to ask Tiresias this question. In a word, philosophy at this time is, as we should say, more pragmatical than speculative, more ethical than intellectual.

So widespread is this tendency that we find it among the Christians when they dabble in philosophy. In his seventh *Stromata*, Clement of Alexandria depicts the perfect Christian; he calls him the "Gnostic". Understand by this term the man possessed both of science and of love. Similarly, Origen draws no distinction between moral and intellectual progress; both together make up the conditions essential to salvation. Nevertheless, as he is strongly Platonist, and in this capacity possesses the vision of eternal Ideas, as these almost transport him into a state of ecstasy, he shows a certain tendency to emphasise transcendent knowledge. As we shall see, his mysticism is coloured with intellectuality.

If, in the final analysis, redemption is the

DOCTRINE OF REDEMPTION 133

result of an education, like all training worthy of this name it will have to become everything to all men. It must make itself different according to the various individuals. Now, it is evident that there are fairly considerable differences amongst Christians. Some are still veritable babes (νήπιοι). Others are making headway, whilst yet others are approaching perfection. The Gnostics were wont to divide men into three classes, not altogether without reason. Their mistake consisted in claiming that a man belonged to a particular class by his nature and birth. One was "spiritual" because he possessed the spirit from the day of his birth. Another had the misfortune to be born carnal and material; he was condemned beforehand to perish. If there were real differences between men, there could be no saving recipe that would be uniform for all. Accordingly, Origen declares that for some "Christ and Christ crucified" sufficed. Let them believe in him and they will be saved. Others must have more sublime revelations; when the moment comes, they will no longer need Christ purely as a redeemer; they will go straight to the Father. Consequently redemption takes for granted a method which differs according to the various categories of individuals.

The redemption conceived by Origen necessarily ends by being universal; it implies Universalism. Indeed, the one outstanding character of a serious education is the belief that it will succeed even in the most difficult cases. A good educator will always believe that, through illumination, he will finally persuade the one whose education he has undertaken, and that, through an appeal to his moral sense, he will compel him to recognise what is just and righteous and to conform thereto. Hence the conviction felt by teachers that education is all powerful. An educator in his inmost soul, Origen was bound to incline towards the belief that, sooner or later, truth would effect the conquest of the lowest and basest of sinners. He looks upon redemption as a return to God. As he says, the end will resemble the beginning. After descending into the abyss of evil, beings will ascend and return to their primitive condition. What reason have we for admitting that certain beings will remain outside this retrogressive movement. The patience of God is boundless, He will multiply opportunities of repentance and tests or trials which will overcome the direst stubbornness. The very logic of the doctrine of redemption requires that Origen should recognise the possibility of all sinners returning to God. Here, his logic is one with his charity. Did he say all that he thought, and believe in the possible salvation of a Judas or of the Devil? This is asserted by his opponents. He propounded the question, and admitted the theoretical possibility of their salvation. All the same, in the texts that have come down to us we do not find any categorical affirmation. He would appear to have hesitated. His case is somewhat like that of the author of the second part of the *Pistis Sophia*, and which is generally identified with the *Lesser Questions* of Mary. This Gnostic writer ardently desires the redemption of all sinners. He dreams of a boundless salvation—which alone would be worthy of God—and tasks his ingenuity in drawing attention to expiatory rites which will prove efficacious in the most difficult cases. All the same, he dares not assert that not a single sinner will perish.

The instrument of redemption is the Logos Jesus. What is Origen's conception of the rôle and work of the Redeemer? On this point, there is a genuine surprise in store for us. Ever since the time of Saint Anselm, Christians have been wont to associate redemption with the death of Jesus Christ on the cross; this is the doctrine that has prevailed, in forms which have varied according to time and circumstance. All the "revivals" of last century regarded this doctrine as the very essence of their preaching, the lever of their propaganda. *Ave crux, spes unica*, has for centuries been the formula of salvation in Jesus Christ. Now, this doctrine appears to be absent in Origen. At all events, though Jesus Christ is really to his mind the very instrument of salvation, the cross does not occupy the central position in his doctrine of redemption. In any case, the doctrine of the expiatory value of the death on the cross holds but an insignificant place in his works. Though the formula may exist, the doctrine itself is considerably modified, if not actually distorted. The theologians and historians to whom the Reformation gave birth did not fail to bring this forward as a grievance against him.

Nevertheless, if we could imagine ourselves in the days of Origen, the astonishment we should feel at first would become largely mitigated. History explains the point of view of our theologian. Do not forget that in the second century it is baptism that procures forgiveness of sins. This refers to sins committed in the days when men were pagan. Baptism effaces these sins; consequently, baptism is designated by such terms as bath, λοῦτρον, illumination, φωτισμός, regeneration, ἀναγέννησις. The neophyte is supposed to come out of the baptismal water purified and regenerated, restored to a state of innocence.

Certain Gnostics even claimed that, at the moment of baptism, the daimons saw the neophytes escape from their power. The tyranny of destiny was broken. The neophyte regained his full liberty, and for long it was not admitted that he could fall back into sin. The second repentance, as it was called, followed by the second forgiveness, was not readily accepted by the Church. Doubtless, in conformity with the Scriptures, forgiveness is associated with Jesus Christ, but this is indirectly. It is really baptism that cleanses from sin. This is the doctrine advanced by Clement in his second *Paidagogus*; on this point, Origen does not differ from the Christians of his day.

He had also to take into consideration a special difficulty. Since, to his mind, redemption was essentially the result of a prolonged spiritual education, he could feel only distaste for any juridical conception of salvation. We must remember that Origen looks upon God, not as a judge who requires expiation for a fault and chastises with the express intention of causing suffering, but rather as a Father who inflicts suffering only in order to obtain the amelioration of the sinner. The test is no longer a punishment; it is a means of education. Hence it is very difficult for him to admit that there is an expiatory significance in the death of Jesus

Christ. Indeed, though not formally rejecting this idea, he puts it aside, and does not regard it as a real element in his doctrine of redemption.

But how does he explain so many New Testament texts which imply expiation? What becomes of such an expression as the following: Jesus is the lamb that taketh away the sins of the world? Or of that which declares that he gives his life as a ransom? What are we to make of the third or the sixth chapter of Romans? Origen attempts first to explain all these texts apart from the idea of expiation, trying to eliminate it by means of allegory. For instance, he compares the death of the martyr with that of Jesus Christ. The death of martyrs does more than benefit themselves alone, it possesses merits whereby others profit. This is an idea which carries us on to the doctrine of supererogatory merits. Origen declares that the death of Jesus Christ had unexpected repercussions in the invisible world, terrifying the daimons and reducing them to a state of impotence. They became "atonic" ($ἄτονοι$). Finally, when his allegorical skill cannot wholly deprive these embarrassing texts of an expiatory meaning, he decides to let them stand. With the rest of the Christians, he repeats the Bible formulas without making a thorough examination of them. Evidently the texts in question do not fit in with his doctrine; they introduce an element of discord and offend against logic. Out of respect for the sacred text, our theologian tolerates them.

What certainly reassured him is the fact that at bottom, as we have just remarked, his conception of the redemptive rôle of Jesus Christ is in harmony with the Christian belief current in the second century. In his masterly sketch of the Christian beliefs of this time, Harnack has proved, from actual texts, that to the Christians of that century, Jesus is, above all else, the one who procured for his followers, first, the revelation of the one true God, and afterwards, immortality after death. The task of expiation which he works out on the cross is scarcely mentioned. Bible texts are simply repeated. It is baptism that brings about the forgiveness of sins. In more learned fashion, the doctrine of Origen reproduces the same traits. His Logos Jesus is in effect the divine instrument whereby life is transmitted to those beings lower in the scale than himself. To believers more especially he is the upflowing spring of immortality. It is also this Logos Jesus who initiates, at all events the chosen few, into supreme knowledge, transcendent Gnosis. In this sense, he is the efficacious instrument for the return to God. Origen must not be judged by a theology dating from Saint Augustine, but by the Christian beliefs of his age.

In conclusion, what is the dominant impression left by this doctrine? May it be that after all it springs rather from Greek philosophy than from Christianity itself? It is even possible that many may consider that it has greater affinity with Gnostic thought than with the faith of Christian martyrs and confessors. Be assured that such an impression would not be true, and that the implied judgment would be incorrect. The thing which distinguishes the doctrine of Origen not only from the syncretistic religions of the day and from Greek religious philosophy, but also from the Christian Gnosticism of a Basilides, a Valentinus, and even from that of a Ptolemy or a Heracleon, is the importance it attributes to Jesus Christ. In the last analysis, he is the key-stone of the entire structure. To obtain a thorough comprehension of this, the first two volumes of the commentary on John should be read again and again. There we should find that Jesus Christ occupies the central place in Origen's thought, and that Origen conceives neither the existence of the Cosmos and of mankind, nor their destiny, apart from the presence and the influence of the Logos Jesus. We should not forget with what warmth of conviction the author of the *Contra Celsum*

DOCTRINE OF REDEMPTION

rejects the attempt which this philosopher makes to underestimate Jesus Christ. One might quote more particularly the thrilling pages in which Origen lays stress on the moral and spiritual influence always exercised by Christ. It is by the life-work of Jesus that he explains the progress of Christianity. To it he attributes the moral purity, the transformation of feeling and the heroism that characterised the Christians of his time. The reality of this life-work proved the divinity of his Christ. In a word, his doctrine of redemption was but the interpretation in philosophical language of the Gospel saying: the Son of Man came to seek that which was lost.

FINAL THINGS

FINAL THINGS

THE doctrine of Origen which we are now to expound belongs to the class which calls for great clarity in the documents that make it known to us. In the *De Principiis*, we have the following texts: I, chaps. 6 to 8; II, chaps. 10 and 11; III, chaps. 5 and 6. It is known that Origen wrote a special treatise on the resurrection; this, however, is lost. Those chapters of the *Contra Celsum* which deal with the resurrection of Jesus make up for the loss to a certain extent. To these documents add numerous isolated texts, more particularly from the commentary on John.

As we see, the main source of our knowledge of Origen's ideas regarding final things is the *De Principiis*. Now, seeing that both the eschatology and the cosmology of our author differ widely from the ideas current among the Christians of his time, we must expect that they would undergo serious alterations in the version of Rufinus. If this translator was anxious to avoid offending the Christians of Rome, and wished them to give Origen a good reception, it was necessary at all costs to mask this divergence of views. A critical study of those chapters of the *De Principiis* which deal with final things fully demonstrates that such an expectation is a reasonable one. It has been proved that the text of these chapters was considerably distorted in the translation made by Rufinus. It is even possible to carry criticism on this point farther than Koetschau has done. On the results of this critical study is based the exposition of Origen's doctrine which we will now give.

What is the general character of this doctrine? It bears but slight resemblance either to the eschatological ideas of the early Christians, or to the conception of final things which became predominant. On this point, the ideas of the Christians were for a long time uncertain; their evolution was very slow and eventually they underwent considerable modification. At first they thought that Jesus was shortly to return on the clouds of heaven. This generation, it was said, shall not pass away, until the Son of Man returns, coming down from heaven to the sound of the trumpet. The saints will go before him and then the last judgment will take place.[1] Soon it was imagined that the kingdom of the returned Christ would last for a thousand years and be followed by a final and terrible struggle with the powers of evil. This would

[1] See 1 Thess., chap. iv, and the Synoptics.

FINAL THINGS

be the end.[1] In the days of Papias and even of Irenaeus, the bliss of the elect was represented as wholly material. A description was given of the heavenly Jerusalem and of the joys which should be the lot of the blessed.

All the same, it was soon perceived that these representations were rather Judaical than Christian. Indeed, they owed their origin to the Jewish apocalyptic. After a time, the materialistic colours faded away, and there remained only a few elements that were to prove lasting. One of the first to take root was the idea of the resurrection of the flesh. The writings of Athenagoras on this point, along with Origen's repugnance to acknowledge the revivification of the flesh show that, at the end of the second and the beginning of the third century, the doctrine of the resurrection of the body had not yet made any considerable headway among the Christians. Then other elements were introduced: the idea of the last judgment, that of the perdition of some and the bliss of the rest. Very speedily the list of final things became traditional and ceased to vary.

Strange to relate, on this point the divergence of Origen's ideas is a radical one. At the time he conceived them, there was nothing to compel him to bring them into accord with the current

[1] See the Apocalypse, chaps. xix, xx, xxi, *et passim*.

views, which had not yet become finally established. He might quite well have thought that his doctrine corresponded better with the teachings of the Scriptures than did the doctrines current amongst the faithful, and that it was his duty to rectify popular notions on so important a subject. Hence perhaps the freedom with which he speaks of the consummation of all things.

His entire doctrine of final things is determined by the principle that the end should resemble the beginning; in other terms, should be a restoration. After a certain time, evolution goes backwards, the stream re-ascends to its source. This constitutes the fact of redemption. We have seen that, after the fall has been consummated and it has worked out all its consequences, there begins a return of souls. This is even a sort of retrogression of the Cosmos, the last term of which is to be the re-establishment of all things to their primitive state, anterior to the fall.

It would appear to be Stoicism that suggested to Origen—and perhaps also to the Gnostic theologians who conceived the "final consummation" in almost the same way—the idea of a cyclical evolution of the Cosmos. The teaching of this philosophy was that the Cosmos will, at the end, be destroyed by fire. Immediately, however, there will spring into being another

FINAL THINGS 149

Cosmos, absolutely similar to the first. The same events will follow one another; the same men will be seen, saying the same words and doing the same things. Anytus will again accuse Socrates, and the son of Sophroniscus will once more drink the hemlock. When the same cycle has been traversed, the Cosmos will again be consumed in flame, as was the first. From its ashes will again spring up a Cosmos which once more will reproduce the former Cosmos. Not that Origen did not formally repudiate this idea; against those who accused him of having plagiarised the Stoics he indignantly defended himself. The successive worlds which he presupposes do not resemble one another; in this respect, his conception is entirely different from that of the Stoics. All the same, he conceives the evolution of the Whole as a kind of circle which brings the Cosmos back to its starting point. This idea of an ebb and flow of things, which calls to mind a cyclical movement, is what he has adopted from the Stoic doctrine; to it he is unwittingly indebted for the essence of his own doctrine.

This brings his conception of final things so near to the Gnostic conception that it is almost identical with it. Valentinus and his school, along with most of the Gnostics of the *Philosophumena*, think that the consummation will take place when all the divine elements that are lost in matter have been recovered, restored to their source, and, as it were, reabsorbed into the inmost heart of the suprasensible world. They, too, would appear to have borrowed from Stoicism the idea of a cyclical evolution of the Cosmos. What prevents any confusion between the doctrine of Origen and that of the Gnostics is that, in depicting the state of final bliss, our theologian largely retains the Bible terminology. There is a savour of the Christian tradition about his doctrine. The description of the final destiny of men, both good and evil, which we read in the fourth chapter of the *Pistis Sophia* or in the second book of the Coptic *Jeu*, is a far more free one than is that of Origen. It recalls certain pagan imaginations; there is nothing about it either Christian or Biblical.

What was Origen's idea of the consummation? This latter is preceded—and conditioned—by redemption. We may remember that the beings of the invisible world, or, as we read in the Greek fragments of his *De Principiis*, the intelligences, become, because of the fall, first, souls; then, intermediaries between pure spirit and corporeal matter; and lastly, bodies. According to the degree of sin these bodies are either luminous, like the heavenly bodies, or altogether tenebrous, like the daimons. It would even

FINAL THINGS

appear, if we are to credit a certain fragment, that Origen, remembering the teachings of Plato, affirmed that certain beings descended into various animal forms.

The signal of the consummation coincides of necessity with the beginning of the return of beings to their primitive condition. Redemption marks the first hour of the end. Bodies are stripped of their corporeity when, from being opaque, they become translucent and diaphanous; they rise to the state of souls, and finally emerge as pure essences, intelligences, spirits. God is all in all. This is the final consummation.

What, then, is the condition of the beings thus restored to their primordial state? What will be their final destiny, according to Origen?

It is not an easy matter to discover this from the texts; indeed these do not always express Origen's true thought. For the most part, they have a Biblical complexion which may put us on the wrong track as regards the author's real meaning. Besides, he seems aware of the divergence between his own doctrine and the ideas current among the Christians. He seems to try to avoid making this divergence too pronounced. It may be that he does this more by instinct than of set purpose. Still, his language does not always lay stress upon the originality of his views so much as one would wish. In order to emphasise them, we are obliged to note those traits which appear most frequently, and which agree with the general character of the doctrine. These are evidently the essential traits. By isolating them from what seems accessory in the doctrine, it may be that we shall give the latter a more systematic aspect than it really possesses.

There can be no doubt that, from Origen's point of view, the final destiny of beings endowed with reason is connected with their stage of development. Origen always distinguished between Christians, dividing them into two main categories: the perfect and the simple faithful (*simpliciores*). The latter hold very crude ideas on God, to Whom they attribute a body; on His providence, which they regard as arbitrary. They understand nothing but the literal meaning of the Scriptures; from this point of view, they are more Judaistic than Christian. They are feeble and sinful; their worship is still too external and material, it is by no means the worship that is in spirit and in truth. Consequently, they will just be saved, and no more. To them, Jesus Christ is simply "Christ and Christ crucified". Origen, however, makes further classifications of the Christians, separating the more advanced into degrees.

FINAL THINGS

In the first few pages of his commentary on John, he sets up a parallel between the Levitical priesthood and the Christians. The more advanced of the latter devote themselves wholly to the study of the Holy Scriptures, in the first rank of whom are those, he says, who "repose on the bosom of Jesus". This idea of a spiritual hierarchy of believers largely inspired his interpretation of *Solomon's Song*.[1]

What will be the lot of the chosen, the perfect? They will return to the state of entities endowed with reason, of pure intelligences, spirits. They will be incorporeal beings. Thus did Origen conceive of them. He did not foresee the objection which his conception would some day raise. So it is only God Who has not a body, it will be urged. The holy Trinity is incorporeal, pure spirit. Apart from it, all beings, however perfect, have a body. Make this body as luminous, diaphanous and spiritual as you please, provided it still be a body, and your conception will be acceptable. You will be conforming with the orthodoxy of Rome at the end of the fourth century. This dogmatic scruple wholly escaped the notice of Origen; he did not even think of it. Very logically and in conformity with his entire

[1] See the following texts: *In Joh.*, I, 18; XIII, 16, 18, 33, 34; XX, 7, 26, 34; XXXII, 10.

doctrine of redemption, he believed that beings would once more become pure spirits at the final consummation. Could Rufinus allow to stand such doctrinal incorrectness in that *De Principiis* which it was his aim to make known to—and have adopted by—the public of Rome? Here again he felt perfectly justified in omitting it from his version. Wherever he could, he intercalated a sentence which reserved pure spirituality as an attribute of the Trinity. On the other hand, so thoroughly does he expurgate Origen's text that no one would suspect its true meaning. Fortunately, in this matter as in many others, the fragments of Justinian's letter and the extracts of Jerome's version of the *De Principiis* give us precise and definite information. As required by the very logic of redemption, meritorious beings once more become pure spirits at the final consummation. Moreover, if we did not acknowledge that this was really the thought of our author, we could not understand the other traits which, to his mind, constitute the bliss of beings fully redeemed.

These latter, indeed, will be mainly occupied in contemplating God. In describing this contemplation, he sometimes makes use of terms that are wholly Pauline. "Those", he says, "who have come to God through the mediation of the Logos who is by God's side, will give

FINAL THINGS

themselves up entirely to the contemplation of God, that so they may be conformed by the knowledge of the Father into the perfect likeness of the Son" (*In Joh.*, I, 6). Then again he adopts Platonic formulas. "The disciples of Jesus", he says in another place, "fix their gaze on the domain of becoming (γένεσις) in order to use it as a step for rising to the contemplation of the domain of Ideas (ἡ τῶν νοητῶν φύσις). The entire passage abounds in philosophical terms (*Contra Celsum*, VII, 46). Origen's boldness astonishes the reader in no slight degree. He clearly draws inspiration from Plato, whom he is not afraid of following to his ultimate conclusions. Like his master, he carries contemplation on to that divine state of enthusiasm which fills the soul with transport. We are on the confines of philosophical ecstasy. The passage in the fourth Gospel that speaks of the vine (xv, 1), enables him to place in one and the same category the contemplation after which he aspires, and that which the philosopher so frequently extolled. "Wine makes glad the heart of man, say the Scriptures. Indeed, if we are to understand by the heart the reflective thought, and if that which makes it glad is the preëminently delectable Word—the Word, I affirm, which removes you from the grasp of mortal things, inspires you with divine enthusiasm, and elates you with an inebriation which is not unreason but which is divine—then it is right for us to say that he who gives the wine, who makes glad the heart of man, is called the true vine. What is the fruit of the vine? The secret and mystical ideas that communicate gladness and enthusiasm; such is the wine of the vine " (*In Joh.*, I, 30). Numerous are the passages which extol the knowledge afforded by contemplation of God, and which proclaim its superiority. The commentary on *Solomon's Song* is full of this idea.

Not yet have we exhausted the mind of Origen. The marvellous wealth of his thought is found in hosts of passages. The supreme goal of the felicity reserved for the elect is seen in their final union with God. The Gnosis they have cultivated terminates in mystic union. This thought is developed by Origen in the first few chapters of the nineteenth volume of his commentary on John. Here he is attempting to define the knowledge of God. Faith and knowledge are not identical, he says. True knowledge presupposes union; to know is finally synonymous with " to blend and make but one with " the object of knowledge. " The Lord, it is said, knows his own. In our opinion, the Lord knows them because He has been blended and united with them, has made them

FINAL THINGS

share in His divinity, and, as the Gospels say, has taken them into His hand ". " To know God in this way is to know Him as Father. Moses and the prophets knew Him only as God ". It is through the mediation of the Son that we reach the knowledge which unites to God. But once this point is reached, one dispenses with the mediator (*In Joh.*, XX, 7). As the Son sees, so we shall see the Father (αὐτόπτης τοῦ πατρός). Elsewhere, Origen declares that it is necessary first to know the Son, and then gradually to mount to God (*In Joh.*, XIX, 6). Without knowledge of the Son, we should not attain to that of God, nor to that loftiest stage of knowledge which dispenses with all intermediary. At this point, the Christian becomes a god; an idea which Origen expresses less often than does Clement. All the same, read *In Joh.*, II, 2, and *De Oratione*, XXVII, 13. And lastly, the "perfect" remain free; they may fall back. Then they would begin over again the series of falls, as we have already seen in the study of Origen's doctrine of redemption.

According to Origen, the "perfect" will not be the only ones to be saved. These will include the simple believers also. All they need to do is to believe on the crucified One, who, as Saint Paul says, is made to them sanctification and redemption. Moreover, it is solely under this aspect that they know Jesus. Nowhere does Origen say in what the bliss of simple believers will consist. If he were pressed, would he admit that they should remain at the point they have reached? This is very doubtful. Did not his system of redemption by education imply logically the progressive ascension of the simple up to the stage of the perfect? He never tires of repeating that, in the end, God will be all in all. How will he be this, unless all beings finally become once again pure spirits, " rational entities ", " intelligences " ? And yet, nowhere has Origen expressly formulated this consequence of his system.

Such, reduced to its essential elements, stripped of every alien aspect and considered entirely in itself, is Origen's conception of final things. Naturally, as thus interpreted, it is simplified. In reality, it was more complex. To grasp its fundamental character, we have been compelled, as it were, to set free the diamond from its vein-stone. It is clear at first sight that the conception originated with Plato. As we read Origen discoursing on bliss and the final consummation, how can we help thinking of certain passages of the *Phaedrus* and the *Republic*? Hence, his most striking characteristic is intellectuality. Indeed, he aspires after

FINAL THINGS

an endless contemplation of the world of eternal Ideas, an indefinite addition to his knowledge, initiation into the mysteries of heaven and earth, in a word, a revelation of the true solution of all problems. He cannot imagine a felicity higher than that which the perfect Gnosis would afford. In the Beyond, therefore, it is his reason more than all else that will obtain satisfaction. On the other hand, read attentively those passages in which he formulates his aspirations; we feel that there is in them something more than pure intellectualism. This is not even simply the transport of frenzy and enthusiasm which Plato promised to the one who contemplates the eternal Ideas; rather is it an ardent mysticity. Origen is conscious of a profound need to be in direct communion with God; to live in God is his ideal. Essentially in thought, granted; still, what he wants is to live in God.

What delights him in Jesus Christ is not simply that he is the Redeemer; but that he is the Revealer of the splendours that abide in God, that he has opened up the springs of the higher life and hands on this life to those at various stages below himself, that not only does he lead the soul to the contemplation of God but that he unites it with the Father. It is this that causes him to have a passionate feeling of piety for Jesus. The admirers of Origen look upon his mysticism as nothing less than a cold and arid intellectualism. The commentary unanimously regarded as the best of his writings was that on *Solomon's Song*. Why was this? Because in this book he extolled mysticism in such fervid and thrilling terms that not only Jerome but many others declared that, while Origen in his commentaries had surpassed all other commentators, in the one on *Solomon's Song*, he had surpassed himself.

Speaking generally, our theologian casts a veil, the nimbus of Biblicism, over his conception of final things. In *Solomon's Song*, he finds an abundance and variety of images and symbols which he has used in marvellous fashion to depict supreme bliss. In other works, he exploits with equal skill certain images offered by the Gospels. In one place, the Kingdom of God is compared to a feast. In another place, Jesus, according to the Apostle Paul, is our Passover, sacrificed for us. Origen uses these images to represent the final beatitude under the aspect of a royal feast, the supreme Passover. There are three Passovers: that of the Jews, that of the Christians, and finally that which awaits the blessed in the Hereafter. This last will be grandiose and sublime; it will be celebrated in the heavens, in the presence of myriads

FINAL THINGS

of angels. In the earthly Passover, they partook of unleavened bread and of the lamb; in the heavenly Passover, they will receive the food of angels. These ideas, evoked by his Bible-inspired imagination, are developed in one of the finest passages of his commentary on John (X, 15 to 18).

In another passage of the same work, the author uses the words of Jesus on the subject of the vine to depict the almost ecstatic felicity of the blessed. At the same time, he remembers certain passages of Plato on divine inebriation; whereupon his Platonic recollections and the Bible image blend and harmonise in a conception which could have been used by no one but Origen (*In Joh.*, I, 30).

This feast in heavenly places, this third Passover which awaits the perfect—are they symbols or are they realities? On this point Origen leaves us in doubt. So vivid is the image that we have all the illusion of reality. And yet, when he tells us in allegorical interpretation that the head of the paschal lamb represents "the loftiest doctrines that deal with heavenly things", whereas the feet represent such knowledge as relates to all that is most material, e.g. the daimons, it is clear that here we are dealing with symbols. When he uses Bible terms to designate final things, he does not fail to allegorise them as a rule. Commenting on the Lord's Prayer, he does not wish the words "in heaven" to be taken in their literal meaning. This is an expression referring to those who bear within themselves the image of the heavenly One. The "Kingdom of God" is wholly interior. The resurrection of the flesh is inacceptable; the only resurrection is that of the spiritual body. We should remember that the idea of the resurrection of the flesh itself was still at that time almost a novelty. And the last judgment! This he reconciles with that of the conscience. As regards final things, the agreement between his own thought and current beliefs is altogether verbal. Origen retains the words, but gives them another interpretation.

The divergence in this matter between the author of the *De Principiis* and the general body of Christians is manifest and undeniable. The surprising thing is that he himself fails to see it. His sincerity is clear, his unawareness of the divergence is not in doubt. He also believes that his cosmology was but a rational and philosophical interpretation of the common belief of the Christians, and has not the faintest suspicion that a yawning abyss separates the two. Both as regards final things and as regards the origin, the formation and the destiny of the

FINAL THINGS 163

Cosmos, the accusation might not unfairly be brought against him that he was more of a Platonist than of a Christian. The proof that it is really on these two points that he most openly exposed himself and might be taken for a heretic, is found in the fact that it was just these views on cosmology and final things which supplied his enemies with the arguments that brought about his downfall. What Origen in his sincere good faith did not perceive was clear to everybody at Rome in the days of Rufinus and Jerome. We call to mind the exclamation of horror which fell from the lips of the monk Pammachius when he read the correct translation of the *De Principiis* sent to him by Jerome. Rufinus was so certain that Origen's ideas on the Cosmos and on the destiny of mankind would prove an offence to the Western world, that he took special pains to tone them down in his version.

The illusion to which Origen manifestly fell victim was a frequent occurrence of that period. In his remarkable work on Marcion, Harnack dwells upon his hero's curious and surprising conviction that he had discovered the genuine Gospel of Jesus. From the first day there had begun a deviation which had converted the new religion into a semi-Judaism. This was an illusion, however interesting it might be. But is not the whole of the fourth Gospel based on a manifest illusion? Thanks to it, the author was enabled to persuade himself that his Christ was identical with the Jesus who had lived on earth.

How are we to explain illusions of this kind, which were somewhat frequent in those days? First of all, by the almost total absence of the critical faculty. This was entirely lacking in most of the philosophers and writers, the only exceptions being Lucian and Celsus. And yet, however penetrating this latter writer, he is not, as Renan expresses it, so firm on principles as Lucian was. He believes in daimons and in oracles. Origen, indeed, on occasion, gave proof of a remarkably critical intellect, though pressing reasons were needed for its exercise. When, for instance, he wishes to prove that the literal meaning of the Scriptures is often inadmissible, he excels in demonstrating the weaknesses and contradictions—even the improbabilities—which they contain. The truth of the matter is that he needs this demonstration to prove the necessity of allegorising the sacred text. His passion for allegory makes him singularly perspicacious. His century is in a state of reaction against the critical Scepticism of the preceding period; it is for this reason that he detests the New Academy, Epicurus

FINAL THINGS

and the Sceptics. Hence it is not surprising that certain men were victims of their own illusions.

Moreover, the habitual practice of the allegorical method was bound to predispose the mind to the vagaries of the imagination; Plutarch is as striking an example of this as was Origen himself. He imagined that he recognised, by the aid of allegory, the whole of his philosophy in the myth of Isis and Osiris, and the contemporary Pythagorean philosophers —whom he greatly admired—in the priests of Egypt! Origen constantly practises the method which consists in making an old text say something different from what it really says. A fine way of accustoming oneself to be the dupe and victim of one's own ingenuity and subtilty! Is it, then, any wonder that he sincerely believed both his doctrine of final things and his cosmology to be nothing but a learned and philosophical interpretation of beliefs that were already traditional?

CONCLUSIONS

CONCLUSIONS

THE thought of Origen is anything but simple; indeed, it is very complex. As we see from a study of his main doctrines, it is manifestly composed of divers elements.

It is possible to recognise these elements without too much difficulty. The first—or at all events the most apparent—is Alexandrian erudition. Origen is a pupil of the grammarians, the commentators of old writings, and the allegorists, generations of whom had succeeded one another from the days of Ptolemy Philadelphus down to his own times. They taught him how a text is built up, how it is explained, and how, by a special process, it is transformed into a vehicle of ideas of which the author of antiquity had never thought. Origen accumulated geographical, archaeological, astronomical and even medical knowledge, which the most famous specialists taught in Alexandria. Although literature, both classic and Alexandrian, had no great attraction for him, he had learnt what a man of culture was supposed to know. Art left him absolutely cold; his nature could not have been less artistic. What attracted him in his studies—even to a passionate degree—was philosophy. There can be no doubt but that, like most of the distinguished men of his age, he was an enthusiastic admirer of Plato. In all probability, such dialogues as the *Phaedrus*, the *Republic*, the *Timaeus*, and the *Laws* were his bed-side books. He became thoroughly acquainted with the principal systems in vogue during his time, the Stoic, the Peripatetic and the Pythagorean. It is extremely doubtful if he was acquainted with the New Academy, the school of Epicurus, or the Sceptics; indeed, he seems to have despised them as being doubters and deniers. No one—philosopher or Christian—wanted them in those days.

Origen possessed all the alert curiosity of a true son of Hellas. He studied the Gnostic theologians and was well acquainted with the teachings of Marcion, Valentinus and Basilides. When writing his commentary on the gospel of John, he had constantly under his eyes the commentary of Heracleon the Valentinian, on the same gospel. Assuredly the study of these early masters of Christian thought did not fail to exercise a very appreciable influence upon our theologian. As a result, to a greater degree than any other thinker or Christian writer of the old church did Origen absorb the very

CONCLUSIONS

marrow of the erudition, the science and the philosophy of the ancient world. We can well understand the bitter lament of Porphyry who deplored the fact that so remarkable a scholar should spend his life in explaining what he called Jewish fables, in discovering profound meanings in them.

While the influences just mentioned formed and moulded the mind of Origen and even gave their impress to his ideas, there is one influence which may be said to have fashioned his soul, his very personality more than all the rest, and that was the Christian faith. To avoid all misunderstanding, this faith comprised the beliefs that were so living, so slightly doctrinal, of the Christians of the time. It is always these, in the last analysis, that inspire and direct his thought. They do not check the flight of his ideas, as stereotyped, rigid and dogmatic formulas would do; rather do they keep it in the right direction. Whatever the form his thought assumes, these beliefs constitute its inmost soul.

Is any proof needed of what we assert? In the first place, the entire life of Origen testifies to the supreme importance he attaches to his Christian faith. In the days of his youth, the ardour and enthusiasm of his feelings created in him a thirst after martyrdom; about the middle of his career, at the time when Maximinus the Thracian was persecuting the Christians, he wrote his treatise on martyrdom, filled with the same enthusiasm, and at the end of his life, as confessor, he afforded an example of inflexible constancy. Then again, this faith inspires the whole of his known writings without exception. It is found not only in his homilies, in his edificatory writings, in his apology for Christianity, apropos of the book of Celsus, but also in his most arduous commentaries as well as throughout his *De Principiis*. From beginning to end of his work, we find the purest Christian spirit. Be it noted also that, while Origen made his own the science of his time, and though his thought did not remain uninfluenced by Greek philosophy, he yet regarded himself as alien to his age. Like every Christian of his time, he feels himself outside society and the law, he is conscious of belonging to another humanity. There is no difference whatsoever between himself and his brothers, he is one of them in the full acceptance of the term. Like them he is altogether pacific when confronted with the Empire and the pagan world, though his dissent therefrom is resolute, even obstinate. To such a degree is this the case that he does not really like the very philosophers with whom he is so well acquainted, and it is because he is so entirely a Christian that he somewhat disdainfully rejects

CONCLUSIONS

the peace treaty which Celsus offers the Christians at the end of his book.

From this point of view, Origen is more exclusive than Clement. One final trait will show us to what extent the Christian element predominates in Origen. No one was ever more aware than himself of what constituted the real power of Christianity. To oppose Celsus, who attempted to depreciate Jesus, our theologian brings an interpretation of the life of Christ which was well calculated to impress a man of that time. Origen, however, did not rely so much upon this interpretation as upon a fact which was of striking significance at the moment. Not without a certain amount of pride does he mention—it was on the eve of the Decian persecution—that the Gospel of Jesus invariably produced the same effects. It transformed men's characters and revolutionised their morals, creating in the mind feelings hitherto unknown; it gave birth to confessors and martyrs. Persecution was to prove him in the right. The conclusion he reached was that Jesus Christ must really have possessed divine virtue. Now, in order to conceive such an argument, to be conscious of its force and believe it to be irrefutable, was it not necessary to be a Christian—even to the very marrow? A Christian alone could be aware of the profound influence, the intense activity of his Christ in deeds whose notoriety was evident to all. Others might show astonishment and attempt to depreciate them; a really authentic Christian alone could discern in them traces of the direct action of his master.

Are we right in asserting that the genius of Origen is singularly complex and prolific? It is a stream into which flow the waters of many tributaries.

The remarkable thing about him is that all these elements, incongruous though they be, blend and harmonise into a living organic synthesis which has nothing artificial about it. The elements of which it consists mutually combine and interpenetrate; they are threads of various colours, though worked up into one and the same pattern.

Do we wish for instances of this? The Christian tradition supplied Origen with an absolute monotheism, but when the very character of God had to be defined, as well as the working of His providence, this tradition proved almost dumb. The ideas it transmitted were vague, even incoherent. It is to Plato that Origen appeals for the requisite preciseness. And so we find that Platonism helps to fix his ideas as to the character of God and the working of His providence. By combining what tradition supplied and what Plato had taught him, he

CONCLUSIONS

worked out a doctrine which, as a whole, gave satisfaction to philosophical thought and came nearer to the Gospel idea of a heavenly Father than did the notions then current among the Christians. This was a manifest gain.

In other cases, it was the Christian belief that enabled him to give its full value and importance to an outstanding philosophical doctrine. It was philosophy that gave him the idea of the Logos. He could not dispense with it. All the same, in the guise in which philosophy offered it to him at the time, it was scarcely more than an abstract formula; in a word, it was a principle rather cosmological than moral. His faith in Christ lays hold upon this notion, giving it substance and converting it into a living doctrine. In this way his philosophical thought enabled him to intensify and emphasise his Christian belief, which, in turn, enriched and gave renewed life to this thought.

As we see, the two essential elements which combine to form his doctrines are not simply juxtaposed, co-existent in Origen, without any influence on each other. They are not separated off into watertight compartments. In those days, one did not see what is so frequent an occurrence at the present time. When a savant is in his laboratory or his library, he is really a man of science; he rigidly applies scientific methods. Away from his laboratory or his library, he once more becomes a man fundamentally swayed by tradition. There are dogmas which he will not consent to discuss—or even to examine. In the most intimate domain of all, he is the obedient son of his church, never seeking to reconcile his science with his faith. In Origen, we shall find nothing of all this. His philosophy and his belief, his thought and his faith, blend together and fructify each other. Thinker and believer are closely united, forming one and the same personality.

It is this character so deserving of admiration, this great Christian and noble thinker, whom successive centuries have condemned and stamped as a heretic! From the end of the third century onwards, Origenism began to incur suspicion, and this feeling was universal at the end of the fourth century. At Rome, there was a genuine rising in arms. Hitherto Origen had been known in the West only by his homilies, which had been translated and popularised by Jerome and Rufinus. At that time, Jerome did not conceal the admiration with which Origen inspired him. Rufinus, with the excellent intention of making him better known, translates his *De Principiis*. He takes the precaution to expurgate from Origen's text such bold expressions of opinion as might well

CONCLUSIONS

have given umbrage to Roman orthodoxy. Unfortunately, certain lines of the preface which accompanied his version proved displeasing to Jerome and wounded his vanity. He imagined that Rufinus wished to compromise him, and great was his feeling of irritation. In order to crush and unmask Rufinus, he undertook to give a correct and exact version of the *De Principiis*; one should see what a faithless translator, what a forger, Rufinus was. The result was perhaps not that which Jerome had anticipated. What people saw in this book was not Rufinus, it was the heretic who was its author. Great was the scandal. Henceforth, Rome and the entire West repudiated Origen.

From this time onward, Origenism is looked upon as heretical. Already Epiphanus had classified it as one of the great doctrinal errors. In the sixth century, the emperor Justinian reflects bitterly on the heresies of Origen. His letter to Mennas is a malevolent accusation, the sole utility of which is that it supplies us with a few extracts of the *De Principiis* in Greek. In A.D. 553, an oecumenical synod condemns the memory of Origen and pronounces an anathema against a series of propositions extracted from his works. A pope forbids the reading of the excommunicated man's writings, except those approved of by Jerome.

This sentence is flagrant in its iniquity. What is more revolting than all else is that Origen's most bitter enemies are men altogether unworthy of him. There is Jerome, who was not only a very bad character, but whose Christianity was so inconsistent. He found it quite natural to be the most irritable and spiteful—perhaps even the most vain—of human beings! And what is to be said of Justinian? No doubt he was a great captain, a consummate statemonger, an incomparable administrator, and promoter of the most famous of all codes—but what a despot! Yet it was this emperor who claimed to be a theologian, arrogating to himself the right to pronounce verdict upon the man who had devoted his life to the spreading of Christianity and had confessed his faith amid the torture of martyrdom! Most assuredly it was not the Holy Ghost that inspired the oecumenical synod of A.D. 553!

All the same, Origen's adversaries and judges are not without excuse. The truth is that they were unable to understand him. Why was this? Because they belonged to a time when a knowledge of Greek philosophy no longer existed. Even its meaning was no longer known. Nothing was left of the mind of Plato, Aristotle, or the Stoics. The very genius of ancient Hellas had died away; all that still survived

CONCLUSIONS

of Greek antiquity was the form of its genius: the language, the formulas of metaphysics, dialectic. Even this latter was verging into sophistry and subtilty. Of classic antiquity, there remained nothing but its most superficial elements. Its very soul had foundered. Now, as we have seen, the thought of Origen is wholly permeated with Greek philosophy; apart from this, it cannot possibly be understood. His way of propounding and formulating a problem, of seeking its solution, is that of a mind moulded and fashioned in the school of Greek thinkers. Porphyry was not mistaken in regarding him as a Greek philosopher who had gone astray among the Christians. Consequently, to understand why Origen adopted some particular doctrine and formulated it in a particular way, regarding it as a true and legitimate interpretation of a Christian belief, one would have to be imbued oneself with the doctrines and methods of Greek philosophy. It was this very acquaintance with the thought of antiquity, the understanding of its genius, the mentality of the true Hellenic philosopher, that had been lost. In the fourth century, all that remains is this verbal subtilty, this dialectical virtuosity which the genius of Greece bequeathed to the world before finally disappearing.

Is this equivalent to saying that the exegetes,

and commentators, the dogmatists, polemists and orators of the fourth, fifth and sixth centuries, are barbarians because their Greek-inspired qualities are disputed? To maintain such a position would be absurd. We do not overlook their merits; their writings and discourses constitute a great theological and Christian literature. Not without reason does the Church regard them as her classics. Nor is it less true that there stretches a gulf between them and the writers in the Greek language—both Christians and philosophers—of the second and the third centuries. The difference would seem to spring from the fact that they no longer belong to the true Hellenic race. They are assimilated—not indigenous—elements. This race has quite died out; even now, the incessant wars, which in the fifth and sixth centuries before the Christian era had brought into conflict the various city-states of Greece, had made serious inroads upon the race. Sparta was but the mere shadow of her former self. Then, too, the expeditions of Alexander the Great, the wars of the Diadochi, the devastations of the Roman epoch had completed the depopulation of Greece. The race is really debased; all that is left to it are those vices of which Juvenal made mockery. Its creative genius is dead. It is an age of epigoni.

CONCLUSIONS

Plutarch said in truly tragic vein that in his time, "the whole of Greece was unable to provide an effective force of hoplites equal to that which the single village of Megara could once have put in line with the utmost ease".[1] In the fourth century of our era, this frightful depopulation of Greece would seem to have completed its work; nothing more remained of the most highly endowed of the human race. To the populations which gradually supplanted her, Greece bequeathed her language, her eloquence and her acute subtilty, but that truly unique power of creation and invention which belongs only to the Hellas of antiquity was for ever lost. Thus did the murderous folly of men tear away its finest branch from the tree of mankind. Irreparable was the loss. Had the true Hellenic race continued to exist, who knows but that the history of civilisation would not have been very different from what it is?

How, then, could the epigoni of the latter centuries of the ancient world have understood Origen? He, at all events, was still Greek. Though he might be indifferent to the artistic genius of the race, at least he possessed that intellectual curiosity which constituted the very nerve and sinew of the creative faculty of the Hellenes. The reader of Plato or Aristotle

[1] *De oraculorum defectu*, chap. 8.

finds himself by no means out of his element when perusing the great Christian doctor. It was precisely his mental freedom, his philosophical boldness, his irresistible propensity to deal with all those questions which a text or a doctrine was likely to suggest, that the Fathers of the oecumenical councils could neither understand nor accept. It was inevitable that Origen should prove an offence to them, that they should excommunicate him.

Even greater was his unpopularity at Rome and in the West. The reason why his homilies, translated by Rufinus and Jerome, were widely read, is because they were highly edifying and instructive, and were devoid of that audacity of thought which we find in his other works. The commentaries instilled a spirit of fear, and when Rufinus decided to publish his version of the *De Principiis*, the result was a scandal. From that time onward, Origenism is regarded as heretical throughout the Western world.

Still, it was not only the boldness of his opinions that alienated from Origen the sympathies of the West, it was a reason similar to that which, to our mind, explains the lack of understanding which was his portion in the East. This was even more apparent in the West, and therefore more easy to admit. The exclusively Latin mentality of the Occidentals could not understand the Greek philosopher that Origen was, in spite of the fact that he was also a Christian. Of such lack of comprehension Tertullian is a famous example. He is well acquainted with the doctrines of the different schools of Greek philosophers; he even appropriates certain Stoic ideas for the purposes of his polemics and of his defence of Christianity. There is no disputing his erudition. Nevertheless, Greek philosophy was hateful to him; he did not disdain to compile absurd and base stories with which certain individuals attempted to besmirch the memory of Socrates and Plato, whom, if he read them, he neither understood nor loved. His exclusively legal mind—for he was a Romanised Occidental—debarred him from all understanding of Hellenism; this is irrefutably proved by his theology. What is God to him? Simply a pitiless judge who applies a code of laws. In one passage of his writings he declares that one of the chief elements of the heavenly bliss promised to the elect will be to witness the spectacle of the torments endured by their persecutors. How far from Origen's idea of God as an educator, who afflicts the sinner in order that he may lead him to self-correction, never simply to punish him and make him expiate his sins!

There is the same mentality—though less

passion—in Cyprian. He is indifferent to Hellenism, both that of his own time and that of antiquity. Even Saint Augustine, though very profound both as psychologist and as philosopher, has no real grasp of the genius of Greece, as we see from the chapters he devoted to Hellenic philosophy in his *De Civitate Dei*. Nor does Cicero, the interpreter of this philosophy, find favour in his eyes. How could these Latins, who lacked the broadmindedness of so many of the illustrious Romans who preceded them, have understood or appreciated Origen? How could they have been pleased by his language and ideas, by his mentality?

The Middle Ages were even less prepared to understand Origen than was the Latin Occident. Scotus Erigena was doubtless his disciple; in more than one respect he is an Origenist, but then, is not he himself an exception? Does he really belong to the Middle Ages? The great mediaevalists are Anselm and Abélard, Thomas Aquinas and Bonaventura. What have these men in common with Origen? How could they have understood him? Not only are they Latin, but Saint Anselm and his contemporaries, as Ritschl has already shown, are steeped in Germanic law. It is this that explains the doctrine of redemption in *Cur deus homo*, which, we may remind ourselves, is based on a series

CONCLUSIONS

of conceptions that Origen had previously rejected.

One thing certain is that the theology which has prevailed in the West from the time of Saint Augustine down to the present day, does not spring from Origen. Still less does Origenism impress its stamp upon the dogmas and liturgy of the Church. Indeed, it is a very curious and strange fact that the most original and profound thinker, the greatest scientist and philosopher of Christian antiquity, was so utterly forgotten, misjudged and disowned by the Church. What increases our astonishment still more is that the man whom Western Christianity literally drove from the fold was one of the greatest Christians of his day. If Origen suffered from this unjust ostracism, did not the narrow bigotry which was its cause inflict even more serious loss on the Church itself?

Has not the hour arrived to do justice, long delayed, to Origen, the Christian and the philosopher? Indeed, due reparation has already begun. After Huet and Delarue, scholars and historians in France, England and Germany have paid him homage and kept alive his reputation.

Should that suffice? Is there nothing we can learn from him? Might not the Christian thought of the present time derive benefit from his meditations? It is no question of a return to Origen, of an attempt to revive Origenism: to carry out such an undertaking would be impossible. Political, social, literary or religious restorations invariably come to a premature end. In spite of everything, mankind advances towards the future; a retrograde movement is unthinkable. Still, though there be no thought of restoring Origenism, it might yet be possible to transpose it for our own use and purpose. In other words, we might take certain of Origen's ideas, strip them of everything that belongs to the times and circumstances which gave them birth, and bring them back to their fundamental essence. We should certainly find hints and suggestions—or inspirations at all events—which might help our own thinking. We should be surprised, for instance, if Origen's ideas on God and providence do not prove striking to many a modern mind. Do they not seem to answer certain of our difficulties? There is not the slightest doubt but that, for many a thoughtful Christian, the world war recently ended has again confronted us with the problem of God. It is not His existence that is in question; in this, either one believes or one does not believe. The real problem deals with the character of God, and with His providence; a problem which interests many others besides

CONCLUSIONS 187

the religious man. How could this latter help asking himself if it was really God who willed the war? Is it admissible that He could be responsible for the awful catastrophe? Are we to believe certain Catholic theologians when they declare that God permitted the frightful butchery for the chastisement of mankind as a whole, and for unbelieving France in particular? Such a doctrine is monstrous; it is well calculated to shock any upright mind. But if nothing takes place in this world without His will or permission, must it not be admitted that the war was an effect of His will? Is not this the conclusion required by the doctrine of God professed in Christian churches? God is not the author of evil under whatsoever form it appears, says Origen after Plato. Could the Heavenly Father whom Jesus revealed be the author of evil? Might it not be well to remember what Jesus said to those who claimed that the Galileans whom Pilate had put to death were sinners above all men? As a matter of fact, Jesus exonerated his Father from all participation in their misfortune. " I will believe anything you like ", said a certain Gnostic, " rather than admit that God is the author of evil ".[1] Should we be less scrupulous or less enlightened than a Basilides? To those

[1] Clement of Alexandria, IV *Strom.*, XII, 82.

Christians whose conscience has been disturbed by the formidable events amid which we have been living, Origen, it may be, would prove a very welcome aid and support. Might not his ideas suggest a solution of the problem which besets us, direct our thought along the right channel, enable the sorrow-laden conscience of the Christian to glimpse the solution it seeks? It is in the nature of all truly great and original thought to be fruitful and creative. At certain moments, such thought reappears and asserts itself in men's minds; never has it seemed more opportune, more living than now. Who knows but that, after a prolonged silence that seemed like the peace of the tomb, Origenism will not bring to the Christians of this present age, the consoling and luminous message for which they wait?

INDEX

Aal, 100
Abélard, 184
Abonoteichos, 123
Ad Colotem, 14
Aenesidemus, 47
Alexander, 123, 180
Alexandria, 21, 22, 24, 48, 62, 66, 79, 82, 83, 101, 102, 106, 108, 114, 129, 132, 169, 187
Ammonius Saccas, 15, 24
Anselm, 27, 135, 184
Antioch, 67, 70
Apelles, 15
Apocalypse, 147
Apollonius, 21
Apostolic Fathers, 70
Aquileia, 33
Arcesilas, 47
Aristides, 16
Aristotle, 25, 44, 45, 79, 83, 87, 92, 104, 128, 131, 178, 181
Asia Minor, 14
Athenagoras, 21, 147
Athens, 21, 122
Augustine, 67, 140, 184, 185
Augustus, 122
Avitus, 35, 86

Babylon, 14, 122
Bardy, 35
Basil, 33
Basilides, 15, 62, 92, 124, 140, 170, 187
Bernard, 67
Bethlehem, 111
Bible, 49
βίος, 114, 132
Bonaventura, Saint, 27, 184

Carneades, 47, 121
Carthage, 16

Catenae, 33
Celsus, 27, 51, 93, 110, 111, 117, 122, 123, 131, 164, 172, 173
Chaeroneia, 62, 130
Chrysippus, 14, 47
Cicero, 121, 184
Clemens Romanus, 16
Clement, 16, 22, 23, 27, 28, 65, 80, 102, 106, 108, 114, 116, 129, 132, 137, 157, 173, 187
Colossians, 83, 124
Commodus, 21
Contra Celsum, 27, 33, 93, 99, 104, 105, 106, 140, 145, 155
Coptic documents, 16, 48, 124, 150
Covenanters, 72
Creation, 77, 90
Cur deus homo, 184
Cynics, 48
Cyprian, 184

Decalogue, 73
Decian persecution, 23, 173
De Civitate Dei, 184
De ei, 18
De Iside et Osiride, 18
Delarue, 185
De oraculorum defectu, 18, 90, 181
De Oratione, 55, 56, 157
De Principiis, 26, 27, 33, 34, 35, 36, 42, 44, 45, 49, 52, 55, 56, 57, 59, 65, 69, 77, 78, 82, 84, 87, 99, 125, 145, 146, 150, 154, 162, 163, 172, 176, 177, 182
Descartes, 28
De sera numinis vindicta, 18, 61
De Stoicorum Repugnantiis, 14
Devil, 88, 135

Didascaleion, 22, 26
Diadochi, 180
Diogenes, 48, 132
Dion Prusaensis, 15, 19, 48, 131
Diotima, 81
Divi, 122
Docetism, 110

Egypt, 14, 48, 165
Eleusis, 14
England, 185
Ephesians, 83, 124
Epictetus, 18, 48, 64, 66, 131, 132
Epicurus, 14, 79, 121, 164, 170
Epiphanus, 177
Eusebius, 25
Exhortation to Martyrdom, 23
Ezekiel, 73

Florilegi, 33
France, 185, 187

Galileans, 187
Genesis, 77, 85
Germany, 185
Gnosis, 7, 22, 109, 139, 156
Gnosticism, 16, 129
Gnostics, 15, 19, 22, 25, 46, 48, 62, 80, 82, 85, 87, 89, 92, 102, 124-27, 132, 133, 137, 140, 148, 149, 150, 170, 187
Gregory, 33

Harnack, 20, 139, 163
Heinze, 100
Hellenism, 63, 178-84
Heracleon, 15, 25, 140, 170
Heracles, 48
Hippolytus, 15, 16, 48
Homer, 48, 61
Horus, 23
Huet, 185

Ignatius, 16, 67, 70
Imitation, 67
Irenaeus, 16, 147
Isaiah, 73
Isidorus, 15
Isis, 48, 165

Jehovah, 50, 59, 69, 73
Jerome, 33, 34, 35, 66, 86, 95, 99, 109, 153, 160, 163, 176, 177, 178, 182
Jesus, 50, 51, 57, 68, 69, 70, 72, 73, 74, 95, 102-12, 117, 127, 135-41, 145, 146, 153, 155, 156, 158-61, 163, 164, 173
John, 56, 57, 88, 91, 99, 104, 105, 106, 107, 108, 140, 153, 155, 157, 161, 170, 187
Judas, 135
Justin, 16, 20, 21, 82, 114, 115
Justinian, 34, 35, 59, 78, 86, 95, 153, 177, 178
Juvenal, 180

Koetschau, 35, 59, 78, 84, 85, 87, 146

Laws, 60, 61, 80, 131, 170
Leibniz, 28
Leonides, 23, 51
Lesser Questions, 135
Livy, 122
Logos, 90, 93, 94, 99-110, 117, 135, 139, 140, 154, 175
Lord's Prayer, 55, 162
Lucian, 121, 122, 123, 131, 132, 164
Lucilius, 64, 121

Magi, 111
Malebranche, 28
Marcion, 15, 25, 46, 48, 50, 57, 60, 67, 68, 69, 73, 163, 170
Marcus Aurelius, 14, 64, 131
Mary, 104, 105
Matthew, 51, 99
Maximinus the Thracian, 171
Maximus Tyrius, 15, 48, 131
Megara, 181
Menippus, 132
Mennas, 34, 57, 177
Messiah, 50, 108
Middle Ages, 67, 184
Moses, 48, 50
Musonius, 14, 131

INDEX

Naassenes, 126
Nazareth, 112
Neo-Pythagoreans, 62
νήπιοι, 133
New Academy, 25, 47, 121, 164, 170
Nicomachean Ethics, 131
νόες, 125, 126, 158

Olaus Petri Endowment, 7
Olives, Garden of, 105, 110
Opus operatum, 123
Osiris, 48, 165

Paidagogus, 137
Pammachius, 163
Pamphilius, 26
Papias, 147
Passion, 111
Passover, 160, 161
Paul, 20, 48, 51, 67, 72, 83, 95, 103, 124, 154, 157, 160
Perates, 126
Peregrinus, 123
Pergamus, 21
Peripatetics, 170
Persia, 14, 122
Phaedo, 104
Phaedrus, 66, 81, 158, 170
Phidias, 19
Philo, 43, 45, 48, 62, 66, 79, 82, 83, 101
Philocalia, 33
Philosophumena, 15, 19, 48, 82, 124, 126, 149
Phrygia, 122
Pilate, 187
Pistis Sophia, 46, 124, 127, 135, 150
Plato, 17, 19, 25, 29, 41, 44, 48, 56, 57, 60, 61, 62, 63, 65, 66, 69, 79, 80, 81, 82, 83, 85, 88, 92, 93, 94, 95, 100, 101, 128, 132, 151, 155, 158, 159, 170, 174, 178, 181, 183, 187
Plotinus, 13, 15, 24, 63, 66, 80, 82, 85
Plutarch, 17, 26, 28, 43, 48, 61, 62, 80, 85, 90, 101, 122, 130, 131, 165, 181

Politics, 131
Porch, 63
Porphyry, 25, 171, 179
ψυχή, 87, 107, 126
Ptolemaeus, 15, 24, 46, 62, 140, 169
Puritans, 72
Pyrrho, 25, 47, 121
Pythagoras, 19, 25, 48, 94, 114, 165, 170

Reformation, 136
Renan, 20, 164
Republic, 60, 61, 80, 81, 131, 158, 170
Ritschl, 28, 184
Roma, 122
Roman Empire, 13
Romans, Epistle to the, 124, 138
Rufinus, 33, 34, 35, 36, 66, 77, 78, 84, 86, 95, 99, 145, 146, 154, 163, 176, 177, 182

Sabatier, 28
Samaritan woman, 127
Samosata, 121, 122
Samothrace, 14
Scepticism, 121, 164, 165, 170
Schleiermacher, 28
Scotus Erigena, 184
Secrétan, 28
Seneca, 64, 121, 131
Sethites, 126
Sextus, 47
Shepherd of Hermas, 16, 20
Socrates, 17, 44, 47, 65, 131, 149, 183
Soederblom, 7
Solomon's Song, 66, 99, 109, 153, 156, 160
Sophia, 80, 85, 86
Sophists, 44
Sparta, 180
Stoics, 14, 18, 19, 25, 44, 48, 56, 63, 64, 65, 79, 83, 89, 90, 91, 92, 94, 95, 100, 101, 131, 148, 149, 150, 170, 178, 183
Stromata, 106, 132, 187
Symposium, 81
Syria, 14, 122

Tatian, 16, 21
Tertullian, 16, 60, 68, 71, 183
Thessalonians, Epistle to the, 146
Thomas, Saint, 27, 184
Tiberius, 68
Timaeus, 79, 89, 100, 170
Tiresias, 132
Trinity, 84, 153, 154
True Word, 110

Universalism, 134
Upsala, 7

Valentinus, 15, 19, 25, 62, 80, 82, 85, 86, 87, 92, 124, 126, 140, 149, 170
Virgil, 122

Zeno, 63
Zeus, 19, 64

www.ingramcontent.com/pod-product-compliance
Lightning Source LLC
Chambersburg PA
CBHW071424160426
43195CB00013B/1794